M-D.

Lessons Learned

May Allah reward you and bless
you and your Family

Dr AbuZayd
9-4-24
(Internist from NJ)
(Translator)

محمد أكرم
١ ربيع الأول ١٤٤٦ هـ

(Author → M. Akram Nadvi)

bought during class:–
→ Kitabul Ilm + Ijazah of Bukhari.
Sept 3–5, 2024 @ EPIC

Lessons Learned

Treasures from Nadwah's Sages

Lucknow, India

Moḥammad Akram Nadwī

Translated and edited by
Dr. Abu Zayd

Quran Literacy
PRESS

ISBN 978-1-7338374-0-8

Published by:

Quran Literacy Press
(ICNA—Islamic Circle of North America)
1320 Hamilton St
Somerset, NJ 08873
Quranliteracy.org
quranliteracypress@gmail.org

Quran Literacy
PRESS

Front Cover Image: Nadwat al-'Ulamā', Lucknow, India.
Cover design: Ahmed Agiz
Translation review: Sumara Khan
Proofreading: Usman Khan

Co-publishers: Al-Salam Institute (alsalam.ac.uk)
Islamic Learning Foundation, ICNA (icna.org)

ASI
PRESS
www.alsalam.ac.uk

ILF
ISLAMIC
LEARNING
FOUNDATION

TABLE OF CONTENTS

INDEX OF BIOGRAPHIES V

FOREWORD VII

THE TRUE MEANING OF STUDY 1

THE TRUE WORTH OF ISLAMIC SCHOOLS 5

NADWAT AL-ʿULAMĀʾ AS A PROJECT OF ECUMENISM 9

WHAT DID YOU LEARN FROM NADWAT AL-ʿULAMĀʾ 11

SHAYKH ABŪ AL-ḤASAN ʿALĪ NADWĪ 15

- Family and Lineage 16
- Birth and Upbringing 18
- Ḥadīth Learning 19
- His Teaching and Works 20
- His Isnād Chains 21
- His Efforts at Daʿwah And Revival 22
- His Works on Revival 24
- The Place of the Sunnah in Islamic Revival 27
- Accolades from Other Scholars 30
- His Passing 31

MANNERS IN ISLAM 35

WHO TAUGHT YOU TO REMEMBER GOD 37

- Biography of Muḥammad Aḥmad of Pratapgarh 38

WHO TAUGHT YOU TO FEAR GOD 43

- The Exemplary Fear of Sufyān al-Thawrī 44
- A Fearful Companion of Mine 46

WHO TAUGHT YOU GENEROSITY OF SPIRIT 49

- Generosity of Abū al-Ḥasan ʿAlī Nadwī 49

WHO TAUGHT YOU GENTLENESS **53**

Biography of ʿAbd al-Fattāḥ Abū Ghuddah 54
Training Yourselves to Be Kind 56

WHO TAUGHT YOU FORBEARANCE **59**

Biography of Muḥammad Rābiʿ Ḥasanī Nadwī 61

WHO TAUGHT YOU ISLAMIC THOUGHT **67**

Biography of Muḥammad Wāḍiḥ Rashīd Nadwī 68

WHO TAUGHT YOU HOW TO THINK CRITICALLY **73**

Biography of Shahbāz Iṣlāḥī 74

WHO TAUGHT YOU QUR'ĀNIC EXEGESIS **79**

Meanings of the Terms Tafsīr and Ta'wīl 79
Most Important Tafsīr Works 80
Biography of Burhān al-Dīn Sambhalī 83
Biography of Muḥammad ʿĀrif Sambhalī 84

WHO TAUGHT YOU ḤADĪTH **87**

My Personal Journey in Ḥadīth Studies 87
Biography of ʿAbd al-Sattār Aʿẓamī 89
Biography of Ḍiyā' al-Ḥasan Nadwī 90
Biography of Muḥammad Zakariyyā Sunbhulī Nadwī 91

WHO TAUGHT YOU PRINCIPLES OF ḤADĪTH **93**

Biography of Salmān Ḥusaynī Nadwī 94

WHO TAUGHT YOU JURISPRUDENCE **97**

Meaning of Fiqh 97
History of Fiqh 97
Biography of Ḥabīb al-Raḥmān Nadwī 98
Biography of Muḥammad Ẓahūr Nadwī 100

WHO TAUGHT YOU HISTORY **103**

The Importance of Studying History 103
Essential References in Islamic History 104
Biography of Abū al-ʿIrfān Nadwī 106

WHO TAUGHT YOU PRE-ISLAMIC POETRY 109
BENEFITS OF LEARNING PRE-ISLAMIC POETRY 110
MUḤAMMAD RĀBIʿ NADWĪ'S MANNER OF TEACHING POETRY 111
WHO TAUGHT YOU POETRY AND PROSE 112
BIOGRAPHY OF SHAFĪQ AL-RAḤMĀN NADWĪ 113
BIOGRAPHY OF SHAMS AL-ḤAQQ NADWĪ 115
WHO TAUGHT YOU MEDIA AND COMMUNICATION 117
BIOGRAPHY OF NADHR AL-ḤAFĪẒ NADWĪ 119
WHO TAUGHT YOU LITERARY TASTE 121
BIOGRAPHY OF ʿABD AL-NŪR NADWĪ 122
WHO TAUGHT YOU LITERARY CRITICISM 125
BIOGRAPHY OF SAʿĪD AL-RAḤMĀN AʿẒAMĪ NADWĪ 126
WHO TAUGHT YOU DIALECTICS 129
BIOGRAPHY OF NĀṢIR ʿALĪ NADWĪ 129
HARMS AND BENEFITS OF DIALECTICS 131
WISDOM, GOOD INSTRUCTION AND ARGUMENT 133
WHO TAUGHT YOU TO WRITE 137
HOW MAULĀNĀ WĀḌIḤ RASHĪD NADWĪ TAUGHT US COMPOSITION 137
HOW SHOULD YOU WRITE AN ARTICLE? 141
LUCKNOW 145
OH STRANGER AMONG HIS PEERS AND TIME! 151
REMEMBERING MAULĀNĀ WĀḌIḤ RASHĪD NADWĪ 151
WHAT ARE YOU? 157
REFERENCES 161
INDEX 165

INDEX OF BIOGRAPHIES

Shaykh Abū Al-Ḥasan ʿAlī Nadwī **15**

Muḥammad Aḥmad of Pratapgarh 38
A Fearful Companion of Mine 46
Generosity of Abū al-Ḥasan ʿAlī Nadwī 49
ʿAbd al-Fattāḥ Abū Ghuddah 54
Muḥammad Rābiʿ Ḥasanī Nadwī 61
Muḥammad Wāḍiḥ Rashīd Nadwī 68
Shahbāz Iṣlāḥī 74
Burhān al-Dīn Sambhalī 83
Muḥammad ʿĀrif Sambhalī 84
ʿAbd al-Sattār Aʿẓamī 89
Ḍiyāʾ al-Ḥasan Nadwī 90
Muḥammad Zakariyyā Sunbhulī Nadwī 91
Salmān Ḥusaynī Nadwī 94
Ḥabīb al-Raḥmān Nadwī 98
Muḥammad Ẓahūr Nadwī 100
Abū al-ʿIrfān Nadwī 106
Shafīq al-Raḥmān Nadwī 113
Shams al-Ḥaqq Nadwī 115
Nadhr al-Ḥafīẓ Nadwī 119
ʿAbd al-Nūr Nadwī 122
Saʿīd al-Raḥmān Aʿẓamī Nadwī 126
Nāṣir ʿAlī Nadwī 129

FOREWORD

'Name your teachers!'

This was the solemn rallying call of early Islam as the community gathered to safeguard the Prophetic legacy from the very real and growing threat of distortion. It was a way to trace the genealogy of teachers back to the sources of knowledge, a process which came to be known as the isnād, or chain of narrations. Dr. Jonathan Brown observes, "[The isnād] became the veritable symbol of the 'cult of authenticity' that is Sunni Islam."[1] Muḥammad b. Sīrīn (d. 110/729), an early authority, stated: "They were not accustomed to asking about isnād, but when the intrigues intensified, they began to demand: 'Name for us your men (teachers)!'"[2] It is in this spirit that Dr. Moḥammad Akram Nadwī has compiled this book to answer this very question.

This is the second major work of my shaykh that I have had the honor to critically translate and present to the readers. It represents the esteemed scholar's preferred genre choice for his personal writings and reflections. I have previously taken many of these essays and translated them under a series entitled *Imlā' al-Khāṭir* (literally, "dictation of thoughts") and published by Al-Salam Institute Press. In these, Dr. Akram follows in the tradition of the Ḥanbalī scholar Ibn al-Jawzī's *Ṣayd al-khāṭir* and shares his reflections on a variety of topics ranging from theology to law, history to heart softeners, philosophy, education and more. Composed in a casual, conversational style consisting of questions followed by brief answers—each portion predicated by *qālū/qultu* ('they said'/'I responded')—he utilizes therein a refined and elevated level of Arabic, reflecting his love of the language and his extensive expertise in Arabic grammar and rhetoric. These piercing reflections are part of the broader balāghah genre within Arabic literature.

So, what exactly is this book and why should anyone bother to read it? Beyond the obvious appeal to the growing number of students, colleagues and people genuinely interested in Dr. Akram, the book simultaneously

---

[1] Pg. 80. Brown, Jonathan A.C. *Hadith: Muhammad's Legacy in the Medieval and Modern World.* London, UK: Oneworld Publications. 2nd edition. 2018.

[2] Muqaddimah Ṣaḥīḥ Muslim: Bāb al-isnād min al-dīn.

accomplishes two major tasks and should be understood as representing two books.

First, it emphasizes key lessons learned in the major Islamic disciplines, each in its own chapter. What is unique is that Dr. Akram highlights his own critical insights on each topic, of the sort that are usually not found in standard texts. Also, he includes not only the usual subjects taught in standard Islamic colleges and seminaries—from ḥadīth and fiqh to tafsīr and history—but goes beyond that to include lesser studied, but equally important topics such as literary criticism, poetry, polemics, and literature; and then even beyond that to include those topics that aren't academic at all but equally critical to a scholar of the faith—dhikr, fear of God, forbearance, generosity, critical thinking and more. In the end, the reader has in his hands a wonderful survey and comprehensive roadmap of the Islamic sciences.

The second aim of the book—and perhaps the primary one—is to present biographies of some of Dr. Akram's senior teachers at Nadwat al-'Ulamā'. As such, he chooses one key teacher from each discipline he has chosen to highlight, giving us glimpses into their lives, personalities, habits and more. Some of these teachers are alive, and some long gone but certainly not forgotten. All of this serves to provide a poignant snapshot of life and scholarship at Nadwah, and also opens up for the reader the Muslim literary and intellectual world of the Indian subcontinent, a topic of much interest in recent times.

In the end, the reader has in hand a critical survey of the Islamic sciences, a book of profound insights and reflections on various Islamic subjects, a biographical work of many renowned teachers at Nadwat al-'Ulamā', and a local history of Indian Muslim scholarship.

The book is set in one great institution of Muslim India, whose full name is Dār al-'Ulūm Nadwat al-'Ulamā', known in short as Nadwat al-'Ulamā' or as Nadwah. It will suffice here to quote from Dr. Akram's previous related work:

> Nadwat al-'Ulamā' was established in 1893 (1311 AH) as a revivalist movement by some sincere, far-sighted scholars of Islam, who were firm in their belief in the doctrines of Islam and who enjoyed a revered social standing on account of their piety and learning. They came out of the school of Shaykh al-Islam Shāh Walīullah Dihlawī and his disciples. The guides and leaders of this earnest group of men were Mawlānā

Muḥammad 'Alī Mungerī, Mawlānā Shiblī Nu'mānī and Mawlānā 'Abd al-Ḥayy Ḥasanī.

Nadwat al-'Ulamā' aimed: (a) to introduce appropriate changes into the syllabuses of Islamic training in order to bring them into line with the changed conditions of the modern age, and to integrate religious education, as far as possible, with the cultural progress of the community; (b) to examine the principles and conjunctions of the Sharī'ah in order to sustain their conformity with the fundamental guidance of the Qur'ān and sunnah while addressing an ever-growing number of modern questions and problems; (c) to establish a library in northern India to serve as a centre for study and research in Islamic sciences; (d) to propagate the Islamic faith and ideals through suitable literature and to make arrangements for its publication; (e) to train and educate teachers who have a sufficiently deep knowledge of the Qur'ān and Sunnah to affect the moral environment and improve the prevailing social conditions.

Nadwat al-'Ulamā' held its annual sessions in different cities. But it was soon felt that unless some practical steps were taken to translate these ideas into action, the movement would not be understood and appreciated. Accordingly, the first step was taken in 1898 (1316 AH) with the establishment at Lucknow of a Dār al-'Ulūm (literally, 'the house of the sciences'). This institution quietly earned itself a proud reputation, in India and abroad, as a modern seat of learning the Arabic language and Islamic sciences.

Dār al-'Ulūm concentrates particularly on the Qur'ān, traditions of the Prophet, Islamic law, and Arabic as a classical and living language. The importance and effectiveness of the endeavors of the Nadwat al-'Ulamā' have been acknowledged throughout India and in the entire world.

In brief, Dār al-'Ulūm has tried to produce intellectually broad-minded scholars able to connect with the wider world, and therefore to represent and extend Islam. To expound the eternal nature of the Divine Message and the distinguishing features of the Sharī'ah and its way in such language as might

> appeal to the modern mind, and so help to bring about a confluence between the traditional and the modern.[3]

In the chronology of Dr. Akram's personal writings, *Lessons Learned* represents an important milestone, in that he first published *Madrasah Life: A Student's Day at Nadwat al-'Ulamā'* (Turath Publishing: 2007) some thirteen years ago to showcase a single day in the life of a religious school, or madrasah. As James Piscatori of the University of Oxford observed in the foreword to the book, it came at an opportune time when the madrasah was at the center of the media spotlight due to global geopolitics. This work served to correct many mis-notions people had concerning what really went on inside a typical madrasah. The book had a significant impact but was criticized as being too brief. Shaykh Bilal Ali Ansari, for instance, observed in a book review from 2008:

> Due to the brevity of the story, the reader becomes less attached to the personalities mentioned in the book than he may like. I personally would have liked for the narrative to have been longer, but the brevity of the book has its own advantages.[4]

If *Madrasah Life* represented one day in the life of Nadwah, then *Lessons Learned* represents the entire course of study. It is a perfectly logical progression.

This project began when Dr. Akram first asked me to translate his Arabic language work *Man 'allamanī? ('Who Taught Me')* written much earlier but published for the first time in late 1440/2018 by Dār al-Rashīd in Lucknow, India under the supervision of Muḥammad Wathīq Nadwī. Embarking on the project I quickly realized that in order for this to be successful as an independent English-language work, it had to be much more than a literal translation. As such, I had to engage in a critical, non-literal translation that incorporated the intended meanings of the original while preserving structure and flow in English. For that, I had to eliminate much of what was eloquent in Arabic but redundant and repetitive in English. I also took the

---

[3] Pg. 3-4. Nadwī, Moḥammad Akram. *Madrasah Life: A Student's Day at Nadwat al-'Ulamā'*. London, UK: Turath Publishing. 1428/2007.

[4] https://attahawi.com/2008/12/22/foreward-madrasah-life-by-shaykh-m-akram-nadwi/

liberty of rearranging some of the chapters from the original in order to make the text more readable. Footnotes have been kept to a minimum in order not to distract from the text. I have supplemented the book from some of Dr. Akram's other writings that are relevant to key portions. Ultimately, I am proud to introduce this as an independent work, with his endorsement.

Of note, some unfortunate circumstances transpired since the publication of the Arabic work—the demise of someone featured prominently in the book, a person about whom Dr. Akram writes:

> You are asking me to give you a biography of a teacher beloved to me and influential upon me. I've had a long association with him and become very close. By reminding me of him, you have ignited great emotion within me, awakened dormant sadness, and rekindled his love and respect within my soul. I find my pen and mind competing to answer your request, and I do not know which of them will win.[5]

It is worth noting that these descriptions, full of emotion as they are, were penned prior to the Shaykh's demise. He was none other than Mawlānā Muḥammad Wāḍiḥ Rashīd Nadwī. This tragic event inspired additional stirring reflections from Shaykh Akram, which I have incorporated in this work.

All dates are provided simultaneously in both the Islamic-Ḥijrī and Christian-era formats, in this order. As opposed to the title 'Shaykh' used in other parts of the world, 'Mawlānā' is the title for religious scholars in the Indian subcontinent and precedes the names of Indian scholars.

I am certain that despite my best attempt, many errors and shortcomings must have inevitably found their way into this translated work. These should be wholly attributed to me and not to the esteemed author. Those who understand Arabic would be well-served to read Dr. Akram's pristine original work entitled *Man ʿallamanī.*

I must thank the many individuals whose tireless support made this work possible. Many readers may be unaware of the incredible amount of time and effort that goes into the publication of a single book, even if it is only a translation. Credit goes first and foremost to my parents for their upbringing and care that brought me to this point. Any little success or achievement I

---

[5] See chapter 12.

enjoy—occasions that are few if any at all—is due to their prayers and sacrifice. Above all, I am overcome with overwhelming sadness at moments like these. Ever since I lost my mother nearly a decade ago, I have no one to share these moments with. I wasn't able to tell her, for instance, when I finished memorizing the Qur'ān, or when my wife, son, and daughter did so. I can only hope that she is receiving her due share from these efforts, and perhaps even being informed of them, until the happy moment we meet again.

I am grateful to my wife and faithful companion Sumara Khan, from whom this project took away four to five months of valuable time. That is no small sacrifice. Also, as her Arabic is far better than mine (which is precisely why I married her in the first place), she does the proofreading for all my translations and points out all the errors, many of which would be a great source of embarrassment for me were they to find their way into these works. Sometimes I wonder if she is the real translator. I am grateful to her brother Usman Khan, who was my primary proof-reader, for his extremely thorough effort and his many valuable stylistic corrections. I also thank Moiz Mohammed for his general support throughout the work and Dr. Hatem Al-Hajj for his advice and availability for the more challenging translation-related issues. I must note that I relied on previous translations of sections of this work by my other colleagues, including Tariq Pandor and Fatima Chaudhury. Tariq is particularly talented, and I only wish his time would allow for more translation-work so that we could produce higher quality works than my own. I thank my friend Isa Kundra, one of the most serious students of knowledge I have ever known, for helping me get a current photograph of Nadwah for the front cover. I thank my friend Ahmed Agiz who volunteered for the cover design and put up with endless adjustments until coming up with the final product. I am greatly impressed by his work and I trust you will too.

Whenever I see a great building or successful institution, I am always astounded by the notion of success and how it occurs. Every achievement is the end result of a complex network of inter-linking pathways and the decisions of countless individuals, such that one is left overwhelmed and utterly incapable of identifying—let alone thanking—all the persons involved. Who deserves all the credit? Is it the ones who actually built the structure, the ones who contributed financially, or the ones who first conceived of the idea? What about the families of these individuals, and the parents that raised them? And what about all the anonymous well-wishers and supporters, and the selfless worshippers who pray for your success in the middle of the night without you even knowing them? In the end, the only solace lies in recognizing that only God is the only ultimate *ḥasīb* (reckoner).

And sufficient is God in keeping the account.[6]

Abu Zayd,
New Jersey

March 26, 2019 / 19 Rajab 1440

[6] Qur'ān 33:39.

1

THE TRUE MEANING OF STUDY

They asked: There is a matter that has confused us greatly and, as you are our teacher, can you please remove that confusion and clarify for us the correct way to look at it? I replied: I have never spared any effort in exposing the truth and removing confusions and misunderstandings from what is correct, so what is it that you find difficult and whose reins escape you?

They replied: We live in a developed age and advanced time, in which everything has become easy and paths are well-trodden. Sciences are easily attainable, and the arts and literature are readily accessible and within the scope of comprehension and deliberation. If we want to know, for instance, the history of a particular nation, the climate of an area, any of the natural sciences, or a medical or scientific theory, we would watch a television program which condenses for us the details in simple, enjoyable language and in an easy, attractive style. In this way, we pick up science and literature through the internet, YouTube and short messages on WhatsApp.

They said: We also observe that you have made level ground rugged and easy matters more difficult. You urge us to emulate the way of the early predecessors and the critically verifying scholars who combined extensive expertise in knowledge with personal practice and piety. You quote to us their stories which leave us amazed at the extent of their readings, auditions, exhausting travels and bearing of difficulties in the path of knowledge. We are amazed at their production of loads of beneficial books which are beyond description and explanation. And you narrate to us about yourself, that you have studied—in addition to what you have learned from your teachers at Nadwat al-'Ulamā'—the writings of Ibn Ḥazm, Ibn Sīnā, Ibn al-Jawzī, Mizzī, Ibn Taymiyyah, Dhahabī, Ibn Khaldūn, and Ibn Ḥajar, along with the writings of contemporary scholars such as Shiblī Nu'mānī, Ḥamīd al-Dīn Farāhī, Rashīd Riḍā, Sayyid Sulaymān Nadwī, Abū al-Kalām Āzād, 'Abd al-Majīd Daryābādī, al-Manfalūṭī, al-Rāfi'ī, al-Sibā'ī, Ṭāhā Ḥusayn, Aḥmad Amīn, Abū al-A'lā Mawdūdī, Abū al-Ḥasan 'Alī Nadwī, Sayyid Quṭb, and Qaraḍāwī, as well as the books of many Western writers. How can we read even a portion of these when our attention is so scattered, our concerns so divided, our time so short and blessings stripped from our lives?

I replied: I do not take pleasure in burdening you with more than you can bear, nor do I enjoy forcing you to distant lands or into difficulty. Had I known a smooth path or an easy way by which you could achieve your distant aims, I would have surely pointed you to it. I am as keen as possible to advise you in truth and earnestness. However, the issue, as you have mentioned, has become extremely confusing for you. What you are taking by way of abridgements, summaries, concise texts, television programs and short YouTube and WhatsApp messages is merely information, and a type of consumerism by which your age has come to be distinguished. What I want to bother and burden you with is real education and teaching. These information programs and short messages have nothing to do with studying.

They said: Explain to us fully the difference between what we do and studying, such that it may benefit us. I replied: Listen closely to what I have to say to you and use your minds to ponder it deeply. Those who grow up in our time have become familiar and accustomed to pressing a button and whatever they desire materializes for them fully prepared—pictures, foods, drinks, news, opinions, conversations, sciences, arts, literature, counter-theories and conflicting viewpoints—without using their minds, employing their intellects, or exerting any effort or hard work.

So all of this that you have seized and snatched is not real study at all. Rather, true study is to arrive at the truth and what is right by memorizing, deep probing, analysis of views, referring back to sources, discussing evidences, knowing points of view in differences of opinion, being fully aware of known and anomalous opinions, comparing between schools to prefer some over others, testing theories and points of view, sitting with the learned, speaking with scholars, drawing close to knowledgeable people, copying books, capturing points of benefit and dictations of teachers, travelling and journeying extensively—enduring evening and night journeys, sometimes by land and at times, over the deepest seas—and finally, perseverance in the face of difficulties, for the one who adorns himself with patience is more worthy of attaining his need.

They asked: Does our time allow for all of that? I replied: Yes it does, so protect it from being wasted. Beware of newspapers, magazines, television, radio, internet, high-end mobiles, smart phones, loitering on the streets and in shopping areas, strolling in gardens, and keeping company with those fond of food and drink and infatuated with desires and pleasures. Avoid forming deep friendships with people and rise above making enemies.

They asked: Who lives this type of life? I replied: There are men and women from the East and West who do live this. Theirs is a nobility by which they tread upon the stars. They have souls that allow them to settle only in elevated lands and lofty heights. I have seen their type in Oxford, content with hard living and turning their eyes away from the pleasures of life. They have no concern but knowledge and no aspiration but excellence. Calamity and misfortune have become easy for them, as if between them is a mutual bond and friendship.

They asked: Are we not from this world? What do we do about its news and events? I replied: Ignorance of that will not harm you, even if some of it may be necessary. For, as the poet says:

Soon the days will reveal to you what you did not know,
And the one you did not furnish with provision will bring you the news.[7]

[7] Mu'allaqat ('ancient Arabian ode') of Ṭarafah b. al-'Abd. See chapter 19.

2

THE TRUE WORTH OF ISLAMIC SCHOOLS

They said: We are your companions and colleagues from Oxford, having lived together and spent long hours in research, study, dialogue and debates. But neither a permanent gulf nor lasting love has ever developed between us, nor has friendship, loyalty or affection. It is as if there were a barrier between us which neither of us can cross or an obstacle that blocks us both. Our bodies are harmonious and familiar with one another, while our hearts are at odds and distant.

I asked them: What do you mean? Are you seeking to expose me, or are you, while pretending to be among my friends, trying to sow doubts? They replied: We regard you too highly to have misgivings about you. We only notice that when we debate with one another in sharp dialogue and concerning serious issues, you turn away from us to you own prayers. We encounter fluctuations and obstacles in our lives that give rise to tremendous anxiety, while you remain patient and steadfast. We get angry and annoyed while you remain calm and silent. We become ignorant and frivolous while you remain forbearing and calm. We strive for increase in wealth, eagerly competing with one another, while you are fully satisfied, content and grateful with what you have been given. We love beautiful houses and luxury cars while you are neither interested nor inclined towards them. We wander in marketplaces and frequent clubs, while you remain in your house and the mosques. Temptations neither lure you nor do any provocations incite you.

I said: Perhaps that goes back to our differences in being raised and educated. They said: We were raised in the West and educated in the arms of its educational institutions. They do have their known merits and distinctions, and are devoid of deficiencies that would harm their name or tarnish their image. The whole world connects itself to us and follows our ways of life and educational systems, so what would you criticize and censure us for, with respect to this education and training?

I replied: In fact, education in Europe and the rest of the world used to be similar in goals and aims, until the Industrial Revolution at the end of the eighteenth century, when a radical and novel change occurred, and a fundamental revolution that was unprecedented. This was a change designed to foster and cultivate the skills that lead to the accumulation of wealth and capital, along with preparing and training young generations for this economic system and for amassing capital. In this scheme, building human personalities carries no meaning or significance. You will find that some of the greatest scholars, experts, and academic researchers that are affiliated with contemporary academic institutions in the West—along with their followers in the East—are not different in any way from the foolish, ignorant and imprudent with respect to submitting to their wants and desires. They embrace within themselves great vices such as hatred, malice, fires kindled from envy and anger, arrogance, conceit, competition for wealth and positions, disregard for truth and pursuing falsehood.

They asked: Your words are true, harsh and painful, and your critique sharp, but are your Islamic schools protected from these flaws? I replied: They strive to preserve their aim as best as possible, at times succeeding well, and other times, falling short.

They asked: And what is their aim? I replied: Their aim is to create a personality of servitude and submission.

They asked: What are the basic components of this personality? I replied: Its foundation is the worship of God and a state of supreme humility before Him, along with preparation for the Hereafter and life beyond death, purification of the self from the love of wealth and position, and from anger, malice, hatred, envy, lying, hypocrisy and all vile traits.

They asked: How are these aims realized? I replied: By teaching the religious subjects from the Noble Qur'ān, Prophetic sunnah and the life of the Prophet, in a manner that truly establishes these lessons and qualities with the human soul. It is also by encouraging the company of scholars and teachers, who are the pillars of guidance and role models in worship, and by teaching the spiritual refinement of the soul and all praiseworthy characteristics, virtues and traits.

They asked: Don't you live in this world? I replied: Of course. They asked: Then why don't your schools concern themselves with subjects that are needed to inhabit it and enjoy life therein?

I replied: Of course they teach such subjects, which are known in Muslim tradition as the 'sciences of tools and means.'[8] They are many such subjects

[8] In Arabic, *ālāt wa wasā'il.*

in an Islamic curriculum, and when a student masters one of them he moves on to higher levels. So a student learns in these schools, for instance, the skills of reading, writing, Arabic language, some local languages, mathematics, history, geography, logic and philosophy. When a student completes the primary 'ālimiyyah degree,[9] he either moves on to the faḍīlah degree[10] to specialize in Arabic or another Islamic science, or he enters a contemporary university to train in a secular discipline in order to attain employment, enter into trade or pursue some vocation or work.

They said: Many critics have challenged these schools, including many Muslim graduates of these very schools who learned its sciences and etiquette under the tutelage of its scholars. I replied: They continue to criticize, insult and defame, transgressing bounds in reprimand and libel. I am as offended by their words as others are.

They asked: What specifically pains and affects you in this way? I replied: It pains me because these critics wish to divert these schools from their true purpose, stand between them and their established roles, deny their true significance and spirit, and make them hollow and empty like other contemporary educational institutions. They wish to limit them by abandoning the task of building human beings that submit to God and possess real character and virtue. They wish to train students, instead, in attaining skills designed to amass wealth and capital in order to keep up and be competitive with other people.

They said: We see you as being excessive and extreme with respect to these schools, without feeling any need for development and reform. Are you satisfied with remaining in an historical museum in the wide arena of modern life filled with energy and strength? I replied: There are many individuals who are entrusted with responsibility for these schools who have endeavored to reform them and develop them further.

They said: What are some of the areas in which they are undertaking reform? I replied: Firstly, they are constantly reviewing subjects that are 'sciences of tools and means' in a serious manner in order to meet the needs of time and place so that graduating students are intimately familiar with

---

[9] The *'ālimiyyah* (literally, 'scholarship') degree signifies the completion of the Islamic curriculum in Muslims schools across the Indian subcontinent. Typically taking six to eight years, it confers upon the graduate the title of 'ālim, or religious scholar.

[10] The *faḍīlah* (literally 'distinction') degree is an optional further specialization in a specific Islamic discipline that takes place after the 'ālimiyyah degree and typically takes two years.

them. These include secular subjects that will enable them to continue their studies in contemporary universities.

Secondly, they continue to develop the capabilities needed to produce verifying scholars and academic researchers in the areas of Qur'ānic sciences, ḥadīth,[11] fiqh,[12] sīrah,[13] Islamic history and Arabic literature.

Thirdly, they are concentrating their efforts to train individuals to be adorned with knowledge, forbearance, chastity, asceticism, wisdom, justice, and the fear of God. It is truly tragic and lamentable that, lately, many graduates of these schools are observed to be lacking in these qualities—and are often described as not being forbearing, firm or resolute; as lacking wisdom and humility; as being roused to anger like the rest of the people; as being as hateful as others; as being envious, competing for wealth and status, and lacking in the worship of God.

They asked: What is hoped for in our era for these schools? I replied: Their role is to produce the individuals whom I have described, who will occupy positions of leadership and management, who will achieve distinction among other scholars, whose remembrance will live on among the wise, and who will benefit all—leaders, the wealthy, the masses, and nations—who in turn shall bless them with love and reception.

I also said: Know that what Nadwah and other schools offer in terms of cultural diversity, intense cognitive efforts and close connection between student and teacher only reinforces in the student great profundity, depth, and the capacity for research, as well as expanding his scope and breadth. It engenders within him the spirit of great effort, resisting adversity, and persistence in virtues and lofty aspirations. It points him to the path of rectification, piety, and closeness to God. No doubt this is a long and arduous road, because of which many contemporary schools and colleges have lightened their curriculum and methods in order to ameliorate this exhausting effort. The result of this has been that students now aim to pass their exams without being involved in research, investigation and deep study; while being far removed from building their character and personalities; and while aspiring to graduate for mere vocational and technical employment—with the occasional and rare exceptions. In this is a great lesson for those of insight and reflection.

---

[11] Science of reports from the Prophet Muḥammad, peace be upon him.
[12] Science of jurisprudential rulings.
[13] Study of the life of the Prophet Muḥammad, peace be upon him.

❖3❖

NADWAT AL-ʿULAMĀʾ AS A PROJECT OF ECUMENISM IN THE EARLY MODERN PERIOD

Among the problems that Muslims faced in late nineteenth-century India, and which greatly hampered their unity, were the differences in theological and legal doctrines among various schools and sects. Sometimes these differences led to severe disputes that Muslims could not resolve themselves, and so they sued each other in the British-administered courts.

Another major problem was the colonial power's introduction and implementation of its own educational system. As a result, the ummah[14] was torn between two groups that came to be labelled 'the modern' and 'the orthodox.'

It was in this context that Nadwat al-ʿUlamāʾ was established in 1311/1893. Its founders' aims were to bridge the differences among Muslims. They set out to do this by encouraging an atmosphere of mutual respect and tolerance as a firm basis for cooperation among Muslims; and by bringing about suitable changes and improvements in the old syllabuses of the Islamic schools so as to equip Muslims with the knowledge needed to cope with the realities of the time.

Among the main policies that Nadwah pursued were:

1. To turn away from the old kalām/theology discussions to put the focus of study instead on the life of the Prophet and the history of Islam. At that time Western Orientalist scholars and missionaries were systematically challenging the foundational texts and narratives of the Muslims and stirring up doubts and uncertainties about them. Accordingly, Muslims had to focus on these topics, and to abandon the old and sterile contentions about theological and legal details.
2. To be flexible about differences between and within the legal schools to teach tolerance of the judgements and practice of

[14] Ummah is the Islamic term for the entirety of the Muslim world and people.

others, and to allow healthy discussion in the classrooms so that the reasons for the differences were properly understood. Tolerance can only be sustained on the basis of knowledge and understanding of the reasoning that leads others to judgements different from one's own.

3. To reform the old curriculum and make room for the study of whatever in the modern sciences could be beneficial to Muslims individually and collectively.

Nadwah tried to produce broad-minded, broadly-educated scholars who would discharge their duty of explaining and practicing Islam in the modern world; who would expound the eternal and universal elements of the Divine Message, the distinguishing features of the sharī'ah[15] and way of life envisaged and enjoined by Islam; and who would do this in a peaceable and persuasive manner with direct appeal to the modern mind. In some respects, the whole program of Nadwah was designed to serve as a sort of confluence of the old and the new, where the new would be guided by the old, and the old refreshed and strengthened by the new.

[15] Often translated as Islamic law, sharī'ah refers to the totality of Islamic legislation and guidance concerning human affairs.

❁4❁

WHAT DID YOU LEARN FROM NADWAT AL-'ULAMĀ'

My companions from Oxford said to me: We don't share your religion, culture or ethnicity, but we are surely your partners in learning, study and research. You have been preoccupied along with us in various academic pursuits, and we have benefited greatly from your academic experience, your deep grounding in the Islamic sciences, your capacity for language and literature, your style of writing, and your critical faculty. We have found you to be an impartial researcher, an honest scholar and a faithful friend. We are eager to learn about your academic qualifications, your real origins, and your cultural upbringing. We have seen you refer all your academic accomplishments to Nadwat al-Ulamā', so tell us the most important lessons you learned there.

I replied: You have linked us closely not only in learning, research and in academic life, but also in friendship and affinity. I am well pleased by that and inspired to answer your request.

I am indebted to Nadwah for not only my academic and pedagogical training, but also my religious and moral growth. I really do not know where to begin.

Perhaps most suitable to your tastes would be to begin from the perspective of language and literature. At Nadwah, I learned verbal and written Arabic until I attained proficiency in the methodology of the classic Arabs in range of expression, diversity of speech, and height of clarity and eloquence. There, my faculties were fully expanded and my skills opened. I discovered a whole new world and found within easy reach great libraries of Arabic language, and great wellsprings and resources of the Islamic sciences. I began to understand the people of the Muslim world, especially our Arab brothers and sisters. The Arabic language united me with the rest of Muslims in the furthest reaches of the world and in various populated nations.

They said: We have understood that you perfected the Arabic language at Nadwa, especially since we heard Dr. Bassam Saeh,[16] pioneer of Arabic literature in Oxford ask you: "How has Nadwah realized such overwhelming success in teaching the Arabic language to non-native speakers, such that is rare even among native Arabs who have tried all sorts of methods in this regard? Explain how Arabic has managed to unite you while your differing roots and origins; your various intellectual, theological and legal schools; and your multiple political and ideological views, have all divided you—and all this while Muslims happen to be one of the most fragmented nations today?"

I replied: This represents the second thing that Nadwah benefited me with. Its campus gathered people of diverse origins and orientations, who were brothers in the ranks of classes and in the educational and training programs. They would debate and argue points of view, taking various positions, but always leaving as brothers. These scholarly discussions, intellectual debates, and differing views only increased our affinity and closeness. So Nadwah really taught us to remain united and in harmony while maintaining differing views and hailing from diverse backgrounds, orientations and tastes.

They said: So now we understand why you have no difficulty in your dealings with us, even as we don't share the same religion. This inclusiveness which distinguished Nadwah is lacking in the West, for our ideological differences make us warring enemies. Our temples, churches and monasteries are hostile, as are our gatherings and hearts. Hatred is endemic among us. Explain to us how Nadwah was successful in creating this environment of tolerance and respect.

I replied: This goes back to its commitment to delve deep into true knowledge and understanding of human nature. Nadwah was not concerned with teaching Islamic sciences, arts and literature in a superficial way, but rather, it was built upon developing the students' full capabilities and faculties to investigate, research, comprehend matters deeply, and reason

---

[16] Dr. Bassam Saeh holds a BA in Arabic literature from Damascus University, Syria, and an MA & PhD in modern Arabic poetry from Cairo University. He has been Head of the Arabic Department in Tishreen University, Syria (1977) and has taught in a number of other universities, including: Algeria, Saudi Arabia and Oxford. He was the founder and principal of Oxford Academy for Advanced Studies (1990 2005). He has been a presenter of several radio and TV programs and author of several books, the latest: Muslims Facing Islam, Christians Facing Christianity (Legacy Publishing, 2008).

independently. Thereby, students are encouraged to study the works of great scholars, probe their depths, and analyze their content in every branch of knowledge and every domain of arts and literature. When a student invests in deep scholarship and becomes familiar with its essence and its branches, he comes to know the various views and orientations along with their evidences and proofs. He comes to know the places of weakness and strength. He does not become partisan towards one view over others, nor does he affiliate with one school exclusively while opposing others.

5

SHAYKH ABŪ AL-ḤASAN 'ALĪ NADWĪ

They asked: You enjoy mentioning the senior scholars of Nadwah, so which one of them had the strongest influence upon you and the greatest stature in your estimation?

I replied: That would definitely be our Shaykh and Imām Abū al-Ḥasan 'Alī Nadwī. I have not seen anyone more comprehensive in human virtues and worth or a loftier example. He surely combined learning with manners, humility with good character, and love with nobility. I have rubbed shoulders with great scholars from India, the Arab world and the West, but I have not seen one more content nor more ascetic than he. The world essentially presented itself to him and he rejected it. Wealth and riches rained upon him but he rose above them. Positions and opportunities were offered to him but he remained clear of them.

They said: We consider you truthful in what you have said, and we do not deny any bit of what you mentioned of the virtues of your teacher Abū al-Ḥasan. We have seen him in Oxford, speaking to us with his beautiful rising face and his bright smiling countenance. We saw his deep knowledge, excellent character, elevated manners, and ample humility. We enjoyed his lecture and were impressed by his ability to speak, and by the power of his presentation and the forcefulness of his arguments. The truth is that we did not know what Muslims meant by the concept of zuhd (abstinence or renunciation) until we experienced your Shaykh Abū al-Ḥasan. What a pure and pious man he was! We wish that you would give us a biography of your shaykh.

I replied: I have written his biography in a separate book published by Dar al-Qalam in Damascus,[17] but here I am pleased to present a summarized biography which fulfills the requested aim.

In our shaykh Abū al-Ḥasan were gathered the knowledge of the Book of God and the Sunnah of His Prophet, peace be upon him, along with many qualities such as the fear and reverence of God, sincerity and purity of action,

---

[17] Nadwī, Moḥammad Akram. Abū al-Ḥasan 'Alī Nadwī: al-'ālim a-murabbī wa al-dā'iyat al-kabīr. Damascus, Syria: Dār al-Qalam 1427/2006.

worship, otherworldliness, the spirit of calling to God's way, avoidance of innovations, passion for purifying society from evils and innovations, spirit of revival, keenness to establish Prophetic practices, and his unique stances on the trials and tribulations affecting the Muslim ummah in the Indian subcontinent and the rest of the world. All of these merits reinforced his status, according to a number of knowledgeable and eminent people, as the premier reformer and revivalist of the fourteenth Hijrī century.[18]

What follows is a brief summary of those qualities that justified this eminent position with respect to reform and leadership.

Family and Lineage

He was the Shaykh, Imām, Godly scholar, great caller, eminent and learned scholar, hailing from Prophetic descent, Abū al-Ḥasan 'Alī b. 'Abd al-Ḥayy b. Fakhr al-Dīn b. 'Abd al-'Alī b. 'Alī Muḥammad b. Akbar Shāh b. Muḥammad Shāh b. Muḥammad Taqī b. 'Abd al-Raḥīm b. Hidāyat Allah b. Isḥāq b. Muḥammad Mu'aẓẓam b. al-Qāḍī Aḥmad b. al-Qāḍī Maḥmūd al-Ḥasanī al-'Alawī al-Hāshimī. His lineage extends to 'Abdullah al-Ashtar b. Muḥammad Nafs al-Zakiyyah b. 'Abdullah al-Maḥḍ b. al-Ḥasan al-Muthannā b. al-Ḥasan b. 'Alī and Fāṭimah, God be pleased with them all. This is the most noble lineage, for it reaches the seal of the Messengers, and then, from the Prophet and from 'Alī it reaches Ismā'īl and Ibrāhīm, upon them be God's peace and blessings. God says in His Mighty Book:

> *Recall to mind that when his Lord put Ibrāhīm to test in certain things and he fulfilled them all. He said, "I am going to make you the leader of mankind." Ibrāhīm humbly asked, "Does this promise also apply to my descendants as well?" He replied, "My promise does not apply to the transgressors."*[19]

The verses allude to the leadership of Ibrāhīm, peace be upon him, and God's extending this to his progeny, except for the unjust ones among them. This noble verse is further explained by the ḥadīth related by Imām Bukhārī in his Ṣaḥīḥ from Mu'āwiyah b. Abū Sufyān: I heard God's Messenger, peace

---

[18] There is a religious notion, based upon a Prophetic ḥadīth, that every century would give rise to a major reformer in the Muslim world to restore its purity and renew its spirit.

[19] Qur'ān 2:124.

be upon him, say: "Surely this leadership will remain with the Quraysh, and whoever bears hostility to them, God will destroy him as long as they establish the religion."[20] The leadership here was conditioned upon their establishment of the faith.

So he was born in this noble house, one of the world's most famous homes in knowledge and virtue. From it emerged great scholars, preachers and warriors known to history.

The first among his Arab ancestors to come to India was Shaykh al-Islam Quṭb al-Dīn Muḥammad Madanī (d. 677/1278), nephew of the renowned 'Abd al-Qādir Jīlānī, who fled Baghdad from the Mongols and came to India most probably in the time of Sulṭān Quṭb al-Dīn Aybak. He held the post of Shaykh al-Islam in Delhi, educated many individuals and participated in military campaigns. His family was blessed after him with many scholars who carried the torch of da'wah[21] and led Islamic movements in various times.

Among them was the great scholar 'Alam Allāh Barelvī (d. 1033/1624) who settled in Raebareli at a place known as Takiyah Kalān where he built a retreat centered around a mosque in 1084/1673. He refused many grants of land offered to him by the Mughal emperor Aurangzeb, preferring instead a life of poverty and independence.

Perhaps the greatest and most renowned of these scholars in later times was the martyr Imām Aḥmad b. 'Irfān, better known as Sayyid Aḥmad Shahīd, God's mercy be upon him, the leader of the largest da'wah movement in the history of Islam in India and founder of a short-lived Islamic government in the Northwest Frontier Province which was brought down by the conspiracies and military power of the British. He was martyred in the battle of Balakot on 6th May 1831 (25th Dhū al-Qa'dah 1246 AH).

As for Shaykh Abū al-Ḥasan's father, he was the eminent scholar and well-known historian of India, ḥadīth expert, follower of the predecessors, and physician Sayyid 'Abd al-Ḥayy al-Ḥasanī, author of numerous beneficial and valuable works. He was the second general rector of Nadwat al-'Ulamā' and a founding member of the institution. He authored an eight-volume work on the scholars of India entitled *Nuzhat al-khawāṭir wa bahjat al-masāmi' wa al-nawāẓir.*[22] It is an unrivaled book in its class. I have had the opportunity to work on the intellectual and cultural history of Muslims in India requiring the

[20] Ṣaḥīḥ Bukhārī: Kitāb al-aḥkām. Bāb al-'umarā' min Quraysh.
[21] Da'wah refers to the spirit and process of calling to God's way.
[22] Hyderabad, India: Osmania Oriental Publication Bureau. 1382/1962.

consultation of numerous sources, but I have not found a work like this, or even close to it, in terms of its precision, comprehensiveness, authenticity and lack of mistakes. May God reward its author on behalf of Islām and the Muslims immensely.

One of the most important distinctions of the learned scholar Sayyid ʿAbd al-Ḥayy al-Ḥasanī was his eminence in ḥadīth and its sciences, including knowledge of its transmitters, especially latter-day narrators. *Nuzhat al-khawāṭir* bears testimony to this. When he writes on the lives of scholars, he distinguishes in careful detail the ḥadīth reports that they narrated—noting the narrations they heard, the ones they read to their teachers, their complete chains of narration and the ijāzahs[23] (authorizations) granted to them. He himself had ijāzah from the senior scholars of his time, the highest of which was from Faḍl Raḥmān Ganj Murādābādī who had narrated directly from the Imām of India ʿAbd al-ʿAzīz b. Aḥmad b. ʿAbd al-Raḥīm Dihlawī. This was indeed a great and undeniable honor. From his other lofty chains was his narration from the eminent scholar and head of the ḥadīth experts Ḥusayn b. Muḥsin al-Anṣārī, as well as from the eminent scholar, ḥadīth expert and follower of the predecessors Sayyid Nadhīr Ḥusayn al-Dihlawī, the scholar and reciter ʿAbd al-Raḥmān Pānipatī and other senior scholars of his time. Despite extensive research, I have not found any ijāzah granted by Sayyid ʿAbd al-Ḥayy al-Ḥasanī to his children. I personally asked Shaykh Abū al-Ḥasan about this and he denied that his father granted him authority to narrate from him. However, granting such authority to one's own children if they are competent is a known practice of ḥadīth scholars in general, and so I have not abandoned my search.

This oceanic scholar, great ḥadīth expert and master historian died in 1341/1923.

Birth and Upbringing

Shaykh Abū al-Ḥasan was born in Raebareli, about eighty kilometers from Lucknow on Muḥarram 6, 1333/November 24, 1914. He was raised in a cradle of knowledge and virtue, an environment of calling to tawḥīd[24] and sunnah, being far from innovation, calling to God and jihad. Around him the Qur'ān

---

[23] Ijāzah is a traditional license, or formal authorization, of a teacher allowing a student to teach or transmit various texts, ḥadīth or disciplines on the teacher's authority.

[24] The central Islamic doctrine of the pure one-ness, or monotheism, of God.

was continually recited, ḥadīth constantly discussed, jurisprudence taught and memories of the struggle of Imām Sayyid Aḥmad Shahīd told and retold.

He studied Arabic language and literature under the learned scholar of Arabic Shaykh Khalīl b. Muḥammad al-Yamānī and the eminent scholar Shaykh Taqī al-Dīn al-Hilālī of Morocco. He attained high proficiency in both speaking and writing that was rare among his peers. He also excelled in writing and speaking classical Urdu, as well as mastering Persian and English.

He studied the Islamic sciences of Qur'ānic exegesis, ḥadīth and jurisprudence and was particularly devoted to the history of Islām, as well as general history, geography and civilizations.

He learned Qur'ānic exegesis from professor Khawājah 'Abd al-Ḥayy Fārūqī and then from the eminent expert of tafsīr in latter times, the pious and Godly scholar Aḥmad 'Alī Lahorī, the famed Qur'ānic commentator. He spent four years under his tutelage. He also learned portions of the tafsīr of Bayḍāwī from the eminent scholar Ḥaydar Ḥasan Khān Ṭonkī.

Ḥadīth Learning

He learned ḥadīth from the eminent scholar Ḥaydar Ḥasan Khān Ṭonkī who narrated ḥadīth from the great scholar Sayyid Nadhīr Ḥusayn Dihlawī and the eminent scholar Ḥusayn b. Muḥsin al-Anṣārī. With Ṭonkī, he studied the Ṣaḥīḥ of Bukhārī and Muslim, the Sunan of Abū Dāwūd, and the Jāmi' of Abū 'Īsā, and developed a close association and connection. I heard our Shaykh Abū al-Ḥasan say: "It was not Mawlānā Ḥaydar's habit to write the ijāzah with his own hand, but he would ask one of the students to do so for those who had requested ijāzah. However, because of his love and affection for me, he wrote the ijāzah for me in his own handwriting."

Our Shaykh also attended the lectures of the great scholar Mawlānā Ḥusayn Aḥmad Madanī in ḥadīth. Mawlānā Ḥusayn Aḥmad narrated ḥadīth from the eminent scholar and Shaykh of India Maḥmūd Ḥasan Deobandī; the great scholar Khalīl Aḥmad Sahāranpūrī, author of *Badhl al-majhūd*, a commentary on the Sunan of Abū Dāwūd; the eminent scholar 'Abd al-'Alī al-Mīratī; the great holder of high chains and muftī of the Shāfi'ī scholars of Madīnah, Aḥmad al-Barzanjī; Shaykh 'Abd al-Jalīl Barrādah Madanī; Shaykh

Muḥammad b. Sulaymān, better known as Ḥasb Allāh al-Ḍarīr al-Shāfi'ī; Shaykh 'Uthmān 'Abd al-Salām of Daghestān the Ḥanafī muftī of Madīnah.[25]

Our Shaykh also sought ijāzah from the eminent scholar and ḥadīth expert 'Abd al-Raḥmān Mubārakpūrī, who authored the famed commentary on Tirmidhī entitled *Tuḥfah al-aḥwadhī* and narrated from Nadhīr Ḥusayn Dihlawī, Ḥusayn b. Muḥsin Anṣārī, Qāḍī Muḥammad b. 'Abd al-'Azīz al-Majhalī Shahrī. This is another great distinction, as our Shaykh Abū al-Ḥasan lived on to become one of the last remaining narrators from 'Abd al-Raḥmān Mubārakpūrī.

Our Shaykh, God's mercy be upon him, based on these distinctions in elevated ḥadīth chains, was keenly devoted to learning, teaching and understanding ḥadīth and observing practices established by the sunnah and by precedence.

His Teaching and Works

He devoted himself to teaching in Nadwat al-'Ulamā', spending a total of ten years teaching tafsīr, ḥadīth, Arabic language and literature. During that period, he began writing in the Arabic-language periodical *al-Ḍiyā'* published at the university. He also began writing in Urdu, authoring a work on the life of Sayyid Aḥmad Shahīd which was widely acclaimed, and heading the Urdu-language periodical, *al-Nadwah,* which became the official organ of the school. He also authored the following works, among others:

1. *Selections in Arabic Literature*
2. *What Did the World Lose by the Decline of the Muslims?*
3. *Introduction to the Study of the Noble Qur'ān*
4. *The Life of the Prophet*
5. *Ḥadīth, Sunnah, and Their Role in Protection from Distortion*
6. *Introduction to the Study of Noble Prophetic Ḥadīth*
7. *Imām Muḥammad b. Ismā'īl Bukhārī and his Ṣaḥīḥ*
8. *The Role of Ḥadīth in Building and Protecting the Islamic Environment*

---

[25] Shaykh Akram: It should be noted that the chains of Shaykh al-Islām Ḥusayn Aḥmad Madanī are extremely high, especially his narration from Aḥmad Barzanjī, which makes the students of Ḥusayn Aḥmad very valuable. So students should seek out these remaining students for ijāzah in ḥadīth.

9. *Stories of the Prophets*
10. *Saviors of the Islamic Spirit*
11. *The Struggle Between Islamic and Western Ideology*
12. *Four Principles*
13. *Theology, Worship and Spirituality*
14. *When the Winds of Faith Blow*
15. *The Chosen One*
16. *The Qādiyānī Sect*
17. *The Road to Madīnah*
18. *Muslims in India*

His Isnād Chains

He has a formal *thabat* index[26] compiled by myself entitled *Nafaḥāt al-hind wa al-yaman bi asānīd al-shaykh Abī al-Ḥasan* and published by Muḥammad b. ʿAbdullah Āl Rashīd, who wrote its introduction. He writes therein:

> Due to his eminent intellectual status and his wide-reaching fame throughout the Muslim world, many of the greatest scholars sought to be connected to his isnāds and to narrate through him, especially since God honored him to realize, implement and call to the guidance of the Prophetic sunnah, and since God endeared him to possess high isnāds and narrate from great scholars.
>
> The elevated isnāds and the great status of the teachers that he narrates from is far better than what some people possess over him in terms of amassing numerous chains from every person without them being proficient in knowledge or strong in narration. A true student of knowledge is proud of and honored to be connected to the Messenger of God, peace be upon him, through the likes of the noble and eminent scholar Sayyid Abū al-Ḥasan Nadwī, may God preserve him.

---

[26] Thabats are "collections in which a scholar listed all his isnāds to the books he had received permission to transmit from his teachers." Pg. 52, Brown, Jonathan A.C. Hadith: Muhammad's Legacy in the Medieval and Modern World. London, UK: Oneworld Publications. 2nd edition. 2018.

Our Shaykh's narration from the eminent scholar 'Abd al-Raḥmān Mubārakpūrī (d. 1353/1934-5) and the ḥadīth scholar Ḥaydar Ḥasan Khān Ṭonkī (d. 1361/1942) makes this isnād extremely elevated and valuable as sixty-seven years have passed since the demise of Mubārakpūrī and fifty-nine from the demise of Ṭonkī. The ḥadīth scholar and expert of Syria Imām Ibn Jawṣā (d. 320/932) said, "An isnād that is fifty years from the death of a shaykh is extremely high."[27] This fact alone makes our shaykh one of the valuable scholars of isnād of his times.

His Efforts at Daʿwah And Revival

His efforts at revival and reform are indebted first and foremost to his great household which had raised the banner of daʿwah and jihad for generations, and then to his religious studies, especially his excellence in the sciences of Qur'ān and Sunnah. There was also his brilliant intellect which did not allow any influence of the manifestations of hollow Western civilization or blind materialistic philosophies. The most important events which aided the development of this aspect of his personality was his meeting of the great scholar of daʿwah Mawlānā Muḥammad Ilyās (d. 1302/1885), which was described as a turning point in his life. He also received spiritual training from the noble ascetic and great teacher Mawlānā 'Abd al-Qādir Raipūrī (d. 1381/1962) and benefited greatly from his companionship and company. He returned from him having joined a believing mind with a believing heart, and combined knowledge along with practice, external with internal purity, and between indifference to the world and its pleasures, along with desire for the next life.

He saw the calamities which had befallen Islam, and the weakness and decline that afflicted the Muslims, and all of that pained him greatly. He began to live the pains and sorrows of the Muslim world and realized with full conviction that the latter ummah would not be saved except through the same ways and means the former had been. So he devoted himself to reforming Muslim society through his pen and speech, travels, public events and private assemblies. In these efforts he traversed the path and methodology of the Prophets and Messengers, Companions, Followers, and revivalist scholars. He realized that reform has successive stages, beginning

[27] Dhahabī, *Siyar a'lām al-nubalā'*.

with the reform of the individual and then of society, and finally with the position of the ruler. He expended the bulk of his life in building individuals and society upon basic Islamic foundations, uncorrupted by any tinge of falsehood. He believed that while the majority of Islamic movements had opposed the West from a political perspective, they had no problem with imitating its culture, civilization and customs, especially in economic and societal affairs. He firmly believed that political independence was not the ultimate end if it did not lead to the freedom of Islamic societies from all sorts of jāhiliyyah and paganism,[28] or to the purification of society from materialistic philosophies and imported societal norms, or to the founding of society on the practices of the Prophets and Messengers.

Being endowed with generosity of spirit, he used to cooperate with all Islamic groups and movements in that which he agreed with, and he despised creating dissent and enmity within the ranks of Muslim communities. In that, he was strictly practicing the approach of Nadwat al-'Ulamā', an approach best summarized by the adages, "Take the good and leave the bad;"[29] and "Wisdom is the lost property of the believer, so wherever he finds it, he has a right to it."[30] Because of this approach, he is widely accepted by groups throughout the world. This can be illustrated by my own experience. While at Oxford I wrote my PhD dissertation, completed in 1992, comparing the ideology of Shaykh Abū al-Ḥasan and Maulānā Mawdūdī. When the shaykh visited Oxford, I presented to him an abridged version in Urdu. He read it, and while approving of its argument, went on to say, "It should not be published because the present situation in India does not permit causing any split among Muslims." This position of his left a great influence on my heart, as he had preferred the interests of Islam and Muslims over his own.

---

[28] Jāhiliyyah is the Islamic and Qur'ānic term for the pre-Islamic pagan period and has been used in various ways by contemporary writers. The best way to understand Shaykh Abū al-Ḥasan's usage is to borrow Shaykh Akram's paraphrasing of Sayyid Qutb who wrote in his introduction Shaykh Abū al-Ḥasan's most well-known work: "His deployment of the term jāhiliyyah to designate not only the pre-Islamic period but also the resurgence and triumph of the materialistic spirit in the period after the Muslims fell behind in their leadership."

[29] The proverb: *khudh mā ṣafā wa da' mā kadar* appears throughout Islamic literature and poetry in various forms. Ibn Manẓūr in *Lisān al-'arab* quotes it from the grammarian Ibn al-A'rābī of Kūfah (d. 231 AH).

[30] These words are found in an unsubstantiated and weak hadīth related by Tirmidhī, ibn Mājah, and others. For this reason, Shaykh Akram has not referenced it as a ḥadīth but as a wise saying.

This by no means meant that he was courteous to the point of being silent on wrong matters, but his opposition to wrong was in accordance with the wisdom and dictates of daʿwah. His criticisms of the Tablīghī Jamāʿah[31] and of Maulānā Mawdūdī and Sayyid Quṭb are well-known. These were scholarly criticisms that did not target anyone personally, for his great respect for the efforts of the Tablīghī Jamāʿah as well as Mawdūdī and Quṭb are not hidden from anyone. I have heard him say on more than one occasion that 'the truth is bitter,' which many people have reversed into 'bitterness is the truth.'

His Works on Revival

It is apparent that the greatest concern which preoccupied his life was the struggle to restore Muslims to the basic religious foundations which had been established by the Prophets and Messengers. He subjected all his energy, skills and abilities to this noble aim, authoring a number of beneficial works which are considered towering lamps in the field of revival and reform. They include the following:

1. *Sīrat al-Sayyid Aḥmad Shahīd* ('The life of Sayyid Aḥmad Shahīd'): He authored this work in Urdu[32] and turned selections from it into an Arabic work entitled *Idhā habbat rīḥ al-īmān* ("*When the winds of faith blow*"),[33] later translated into English as *Life Sketch of Syed Ahmed Shahid*.[34] This work includes a biography of the great leader of the daʿwah and jihad movement in the Indian subcontinent. He and his associates had served as the preeminent model of faith, truthfulness, sincerity, and sacrifice in the region. They struggled to implement Islam and to purify Islamic societies from evils, innovations, and from the remnants of paganism. They exerted their lives and most precious possessions in the path of God, yearning for martyrdom. This was a book that inspires the soul to great resolve and courage, and the heart to sincerity and great love for God. For

[31] Religious missionary movement founded in India in 1925 by Mawlānā Muḥammad Ilyās (d. 1302/1885) that has a world-wide following in nearly every country of the world today.
[32] Lucknow, India: Majlis Taḥqīqāt o Nashriyāt Islām. New edition. 1432/2011.
[33] Raebareli, India: Dār 'Arafāt. 1989.
[34] Lucknow, India: Zia Publications. 1394/1974.

me personally, this is the most influential of his books. Whenever I read it, I feel and enjoy every scene and moment, and my eyes flow with tears at many portions.

2. *Rijāl al-fikr wa al-da'wah* (Published in English under the title: *Saviors of Islamic Spirit*):[35] This is a work of four volumes which began as a series of lectures delivered at the University of Damascus in 1374/1955 that reviews the history of revival and reform over generations. The first volume includes the first Islamic generation, from 'Umar b. 'Abd al-'Azīz and Ḥasan al-Baṣrī to Imām Ghazālī and 'Abd al-Qādir Jīlānī. The second volume is exclusively devoted to Ibn Taymiyyah, the third to Imām Aḥmad b. 'Abd al-Aḥad al-Sirhindī of India, and the fourth to Imām Aḥmad b. 'Abd al-Raḥīm of Delhi (better known as Shāh Walīullah). Dr. Muṣṭafā Sibā'ī wrote in its introduction: "This book which we present today to Arabic readers represents a clear picture of the revival-minded thought of Shaykh Nadwī and his deep understanding of Islamic history and of the pure, shining spirit of Islām and what afflicted it in later times in terms of confusion and deviations. This book bridged a gap in the study of Islamic history and fulfilled a genuine need. We can now talk about the history of revival in the political, religious and economic life of Muslims through moments in the past history of Islam, as is now presented in a clear fashion through the best leaders of Islamic reform since the Umayyad period."
3. *Madhā khasira al-'ālam bi inḥiṭāṭ al-muslimīn* ('What the world lost with the decline of the Muslims'):[36] This is a unique book in its discipline. It was the first book to say, forthrightly and frankly, that the progress of Islamic civilization was a bounty and blessing for the whole world and its decline and fall a loss for them. It re-awakened Muslims' confidence in their own faith, culture, civilization and history. No caller to Islam or reformer could dispense with it, and it is mandatory reading for anyone concerned with the affairs of Islam and Muslims. In a conversation I had with some Arabs, one of them

---

[35] The Arabic edition has been published numerous times, including the following: Damascus,. Syria: Dār Ibn Kathīr. 3rd edition. 1428/2007. The English has been published numerous times, including (Karachi, Pakistan: Darul-Ishaat. 1994), and most recently as a revision by Abdur-Raḥmān Ibn Yūsuf Mangera (London, UK: Whte Thread Press. 2015.).

[36] Egypt: Maktabat al-Īmān. n.d.

said, "It is incumbent upon every Muslim to read *Madhā khasira al-ʿālam.*" When I later related this to Shaykh Abū al-Ḥasan, he said jokingly, "Then I too will read it." Sayyid Quṭb states in his introduction to the book, "This is one of the best books that I have read on the subject, both in the past and present. . . The distinguishing characteristic of this book is its deep understanding of the fundamentals of the Islamic spirit in its comprehensive breadth. For this reason, it is considered a model not just for religious and social research alone, but it is indeed for all of history as it ought to be written from an Islamic perspective."

4. *Qaṣaṣ al-anbiyāʾ* ('Stories of the Prophets'):[37] Perhaps many of us would find it strange to include a book that was authored in order to teach children in a list of the author's revivalist works. But if revival means presenting the faith in its purest form as lived by the Prophets and Messengers, then this book is among the most important with respect to building a pure Islamic society, especially considering that training the youth is the very first brick in the raising of this building. This book plants tawḥīd in the heart and inspires the self to love the Prophets and Messengers and to hate shirk,[38] idolatry, disbelief and disobedience. It presents the Prophets and Messengers as true models for the human race. It reviews the history of the true leader of tawḥīd, Ibrāhīm and his pure family in full clarity. The book begins with these enduring stories that shake the senses with the title 'Who broke the idols?' Every time I come across this title, I recall Ibrāhīm destroying every idol and statue in past and present times of jāhiliyyah. The book begins with breaking the idols, the story of the sacrifice, and the building of the first house of worship for mankind. The book is filled with īmān and tawḥīd, and rejection of shirk in all its manifestations. It contains love for the leaders of tawḥīd, and inspires every father to begin teaching his children tawḥīd. This book is unique in its class. Sayyid Quṭb states in his introduction to the book, "I have read many books for children and what they contain from the stories of Prophets, and even participated in authoring a series on religious stories for children in Egypt, taking from the Qur'ān to aid in that. But I feel, without any

[37] Leicester, UK: UK Islamic Academy. First published 1990. Revised 2011.
[38] Shirk refers to associating partners with God in any shape or form.

pretense, that the word of Sayyid Abū al-Ḥasan in compiling these stories is far more complete, for it contains deep instructions and revealing explanations that further the aim of the stories, events and occurrences. It also contains explanatory remarks within the stories. These inspire the realities of faith in the mind, until they settle into the hearts of the young and old alike."

The Place of the Sunnah in Islamic Revival

He had a strong sense of the central role that the sunnah played in the revival of Islam and in protecting society from innovations and deviations. I would like to share a selection of some of his writings on this perspective.

1. *Al-Imām Muḥammad b. Ismāʿīl al-Bukhārī wa kitābuhū ṣaḥīḥ al-Bukhārī*[39] ('Imām Muḥammad b. Ismāʿīl al-Bukhārī and His Book Ṣaḥīḥ Bukhārī'): This was a lecture our Shaykh delivered at the Imām Bukhārī Conference which was organized by the Oxford Centre for Islamic Studies on October 23-24, 1414/1993 in Samarqand. He began the lecture with the following: "As to what follows, surely the great Messenger, peace be upon him, is the sole personality among the Messengers and leaders about whom we know a great detail, including the details of his character, personal habits, inclinations, aspirations, statements and actions. We know more about him than we know about many of the more recently departed personalities—and even more than many living ones. All of this is possible by virtue of the tradition of ḥadīth which have been recorded by this great and blessed life (Bukhārī)." He then began to expound on the historical movement for the documentation and preservation of ḥadīth in an unparalleled way, as well as the role of ḥadīth in the rectification of the ummah. He also spoke of the status and genius of Imām Muḥammad b. Ismāʿīl al-Bukhārī in the discipline of ḥadīth, the distinctions and virtues of his Ṣaḥīḥ compilation, and the devotion of the ummah to it, in terms of learning it, transmitting it, explaining it, and teaching it. He spoke of the unique features of his chapter divisions and uncovered some their secrets and hidden

[39] Raebareli, India: Dār ʿArafāt. 1414/1993.

insights. He spoke of the reverence of Imām Bukhārī for Prophetic ḥadīth. Finally, he spoke of the need of the ummah for ḥadīth and its role in the accountability of the ummah, in the movements for revival and new research. He states: "Whoever reviews Islamic history will come to know that had it not been for the preserved sunnah and the transmitted ḥadīth, it would not have been possible to rectify Islamic society, and reformers and revivalists could not have arisen in every place and time to distinguish between sunnah and innovation, between truth and falsehood, and between good and evil. Ḥadīth is an eternal and perpetual school, which continues to graduate reformers and revivalists, and a powerful force that continues to push forward, to bear the burdens of da'wah and accountability."

2. *Dawr al-ḥadīth fī takwīn al-manākh al-islāmī wa ṣiyānatihī* ('The role of ḥadīth in building and protecting the Islamic environment.'):[40] When Shaykh Abū al-Ḥasan sent this book to the great ḥadīth scholar 'Abd al-Fattāḥ Abū Ghuddah, he wrote back to him: "What an enjoyment I experienced reading this! I recalled what the great ḥadīth scholar 'Abdullah b. 'Umar said about his teacher the Follower, noble Imām, and shaykh of Madīnah Yaḥyā b. Sa'īd al-Anṣārī, 'When Yaḥyā b. Sa'īd related [ḥadīth] to us, it was as if pearls were flowing.' I swear by God, your writing is like this. Praise be to God who gave rise to you, stood you upright among us and gave you strength. We see in you shining pages from our glorious intellectual history and from our great predecessors and scholars. You continue to be a lofty example to remind us of these predecessors in whose hearts God planted His love, and through that love made people love them. It is not strange at all that you are like that, for the branches of the noble tree continue to flourish in resplendent colors, fragrant in every time and place."
3. *Al-Madkhal ilā dirāsāt al-ḥadīth al-nabawī al-sharīf*:[41] He states, speaking about the care of this ummah for the sunnah of its Prophet, peace be upon him: "The study of ḥadīth is a science to which God guided the Muslim community in its early periods to pay

[40] Lucknow, India: Nadwat al-'Ulamā'. 2nd edition. 1410/1989.

[41] Translated into English by Adil Salahi: *Ḥadīth Status and Role: An Introduction to the Prophet's Tradition.* Leicester, UK: UK Islamic Academy. 1426/2005.

much attention to. Thus, the Muslim community has worked hard to preserve, document, and disseminate it, as well as to collect, check and ensure the accuracy of every ḥadīth attributed to the Prophet, peace be upon him. Indeed, it has given much attention to every discipline and branch of study related to ḥadīth. This clear guidance reflects God's wisdom and the special care He attached to the preservation and perfection of the Islamic faith."[42]

He also said, emphasizing the role of ḥadīth in the accounting and protection of the ummah: "The ḥadīth also provides an accurate barometer for reformers to evaluate the trends prevailing in their community so as to determine the extent of any deviation in the course it follows. An appropriate balance in morality, manners and actions can only be achieved through the Qur'ān and ḥadīth combined. This is the only way to fill the vacuum that occurred when God's Messenger, peace be upon him, passed away. Such a vacuum is part of God's law in this life. God states, *'Muḥammad is no more than a messenger, and many Messengers have passed before him.'*[43] He also states, *'You will surely die, and they will also die.'*[44] The Hadith provides an accurate representation of a perfectly balanced life. It outlines detailed directives by the Prophet, peace be upon him, that are full of wisdom, and rulings that the Prophet applied to Islamic society. Without these, the Muslim community would have erred so as to either indulge in excess or be complacent. Thus, imbalance would have prevailed. Furthermore, we would have lost the practical example God has required us to follow: 'You have indeed in the Messenger of God an excellent role model;' and 'Say: if you love God then follow me, and God will love you.'"[45]

He also said, stressing that the symbol of the sunnah remains elevated despite the attempts of suspicious groups to sow doubts regarding the authority of the ḥadīth: "The ḥadīth continues to enjoy in-depth scholarly attention, with its treasures being thoroughly checked and old manuscripts being published. It provides the guiding light with which to judge social norms and

---

[42] Pg. 10. *Ḥadīth Status and Role.*
[43] Qur'ān 3:144.
[44] Qur'ān 39:30.
[45] *Ibid.* pg. 12-13.

practices in the Muslim community. It motivates Muslims to attend to their duty of enjoining right and preventing wrong, refuting deviation in religious matters and rejecting the blind imitation of the values and practices of Western civilization. Indeed it is only through the Sunnah that the Muslim community can preserve its identity. It can resist being intellectually and culturally swallowed up by the Western way of life. It can refuse to adopt such a way of life in totality without examining its details and rejecting its elements that are contrary to Islamic values. The Prophet, peace be upon him, informed us: 'A group of my ummah will always be upon the truth until the Day of Judgment.' Those who continue to cast doubt on the authority of the ḥadīth and reject the Sunnah fit the image drawn by an old Arab poet, in which a deer tries to remove a solid rock by repeatedly hitting it with his horns. The rock remains solidly in place, but all that the deer achieves is to injure himself."[46]

Accolades from Other Scholars

Shaykh 'Abd al-Fattāḥ Abū Ghuddah described him in his book *Ṣafaḥāt min ṣabr al-'ulamā'* in the following words: "He is one of the senior figures of the era of divinely-guided scholars and a righteous role-model. He is one of the most famous scholars, du'āt,[47] guides and thinkers. He is the great scholar, outstanding mujāhid,[48] and inviter towards God through his very existence, words, and actions. When he writes or speaks, he provides food to the hearts and souls, and illuminates the intellects and minds. He is our Mawlānā, a man of virtue and excellence, Shaykh Abū al-Ḥasan 'Alī Nadwī."

Shaykh Yūsuf al-Qaraḍāwī wrote the following about him:

> I testify that I love him, and I hope that is for the sake of God. I loved him for his abstinence, sincerity and devotion. I loved him for his balance and moderation. I loved him for the fact that his thinking was free from all falsehood, his heart free from jealousy, his belief free from all forms of polytheism, his

---

[46] *Ibid.* pg. 76-77.

[47] Caller to God.

[48] Mujāhid refers to one who engages in jihad, a term for the Islamic struggle in all its forms.

worship free from all forms of innovation, and his tongue free from accusations and insinuations.

I loved him for he was frequently engrossed in weighty issues rather than bothering with minor matters, with realities as opposed to appearances, with meanings as opposed to results, and with depth as opposed to the superficial.

I am not the only one who loved the great shaykh. I think that every person that knew him and was close to him loved him in accordance with their knowledge of him and their proximity to him . . . There is nothing surprising in people differing about certain scholars, but they are all unanimous about Abū al-Ḥasan Nadwī.

Our shaykh, the eminent scholar and ḥadīth expert Muḥammad b. ʿAlawī al-Mālikī informed me in a writing addressed to me from Makkah that his own father, who was the ḥadīth expert of his era, wrote a letter to Shaykh Abū al-Ḥasan Nadwī and addressed him with the words, 'My master, the shining moon, renowned and exalted, follower of the predecessors and blessing for the later ones, our master Sayyid Abū al-Ḥasan, may God bless him, exalt Islām with his pen and tongue, and cause wisdom to gush forth from his heart and fingertips, Amīn."

His Passing

Shaykh Abū al-Ḥasan completed his life filled with noble deeds in the field of daʿwah and revival until God decreed his passing on Friday the 23rd of blessed Ramadan 1420/1999. He died prior to the Jumuʿah prayer while reciting the verse, *"Give them glad tidings of forgiveness and a great reward."*[49] His funeral prayer was performed after the 'Ishā' prayer, and he was buried in the family cemetery.

His death was a grave loss which touched Muslims of all classes in distant lands from east to west. It shook the pillars of faith and shocked its followers. Ears became numb and tears flowed. By God, it was one of the greatest misfortunes and overwhelming events. He was an anchor for Islam and Muslims, and a great source of support for the previous two generations. His

[49] Qur'ān 36:11.

presence was a source of beauty for the world, and splendor for Nadwat al-'Ulamā'. He was a source of pride and distinction for India, a great link to the Arab world, and a refuge for the entire Muslim world. In fact, all people who knew him considered him a companion and derived great benefit from him.

He was unparalleled and unique in his time, the Imām of his age. He had a combination of virtues I have never seen within one person. He was a refuge for people from their troubles, and for the scholars from their difficulties. Many were those who would travel to him. In Arabic language, he was a eminent linguist, capable writer, and eloquent speaker, without dispute. He was full of insight into the secrets of God's Book, and fully cognizant of its real meanings and interpretations. He upheld its rights and recited it day and night. He was a follower of the sunnah of the Chosen Prophet, peace be upon him, and walked in his footsteps. He was a critical researcher, with extreme eloquence and intelligence. He used the best modes of expression, was gentle in his speech and excellent in his conduct. He was forbearing, always smiling, and greatly devout. He was a role model for the pious and worshipful ones. He had great honor and rank that was well-deserved, and he possessed such beauty, gracefulness, and charm that would exhaust all expression.

His virtues were far greater than described. His learning spread far and wide, until his works filled the horizons in a bulk of the world's languages. With his death, a great source of knowledge and a lofty role model was lost forever.

Imām Abū al-Ḥasan Nadwī informed us: the eminent scholar Ḥaydar Ḥasan Khān Ṭonkī informed us: the eminent scholar Ḥusayn b. Muḥsin al-Anṣārī informed us: Muḥammad b. Nāṣir al-Ḥāzimī informed us: al-Wajīh 'Abd al-Raḥmān b. Sulaymān al-Ahdal informed us: the ḥadīth expert Muḥammad Murtaḍā al-Zabīdī informed us: Sābiq b. Ramaḍān informed us: al-Shams al-Bābilī informed us: al-Shams Muḥammad al-Ramlī informed us: Qāḍī Zakariyyā' al-Anṣārī informed us: Muḥammad b. Muqbil informed us: al-Ṣalāḥ b. Abū 'Umar informed us: al-Fakhr b. al-Bukhārī informed us: Qāḍī Abū al-Makārim Aḥmad b. Muḥammad al-Lubbān and Abū Ja'far Muḥammad b. Aḥmad al-Ṣaydalānī both informed us: Abū 'Alī al-Ḥaddād informed us: Abū Na'īm al-Ḥāfiẓ informed us: Abū Bakr b. Yūsuf narrated to us: al-Ḥārith b. Muḥammad b. Abū Usāmah narrated to us: Muḥammad b. 'Abdullah b. Kināsah narrated to us: Hishām b. 'Urwah narrated to us from his father: from 'Abdullah b. 'Amr b. al-'Āṣ: from the Prophet, peace be upon him, who said:

"God does not take away knowledge by removing it from (the hearts of) people, but takes it away by the death of the scholars, until none of them remain and people begin to take as their leaders ignorant persons who when consulted will give their verdict without knowledge. So they will go astray and will lead the people astray."[50]

Ibn Ḥajar states in his comments on this ḥadīth: The Prophet said these words during the Farewell Pilgrimage, as narrated by Aḥmad and Ṭabarānī from the ḥadīth of Abū Umāmah, who said: The Prophet, peace be upon him, said during the Farewell Pilgrimage: "Take knowledge before it is lifted or taken away." A bedouin asked, "How will it be lifted?" He replied, "Verily the departure of knowledge is through the departure of those who carried it." The Prophet repeated this three times.[51]

Ibn Ḥajar also said: Aḥmad also related from Ibn Mas'ūd who said: "Do you know what the departure of knowledge is? It is the passing of the scholars." The previously mentioned ḥadīth of Abū Umāmah informs us of the chronology of this ḥadīth. It also teaches us that the existence of books after the passing of scholars will not benefit those who are not scholars in any way. The Bedouin had asked the Prophet: "How would knowledge be lifted when the copies of the Qur'ān are with us? We learn from them and teach that to our women, children and servants." The Prophet lifted his head in a state of anger and said, "These Jews and Christians have their books among themselves, but they are not connected to even a tiny portion of what their Prophets had brought to them."[52]

O seekers of knowledge, take knowledge from its practitioners before they are gone! Learn from them the sunnah, behavior, wisdom and Islamic manners before they pass away. This knowledge can only be taken from those who practice it, and from those who are guided by its directives and ethics, following the practices of the Prophets and Messengers, combining between piety, abstinence and sincerity. Such people are few indeed!

---

[50] Ṣaḥīḥ Bukhārī: Kitāb al-'Ilm. Bāb kayfa yaqbiḍu al-'ilm. Also in Kitāb al-I'tiṣām. Bāb mā yudhkar fi dhamm al-ra'y wa takalluf al-qiyās. Here, Dr. Akram Nadwī is quoting this particular ḥadīth with its full isnād (chain of narrators) from his teacher Shaykh Abū al-Ḥasan to Imām Bukhārī and ultimately to the Prophet.

[51] Ibn Ḥajar, *Fatḥ al-Bārī.*

[52] *Ibid.*

6

MANNERS IN ISLAM

Our manners are, after our skin, and then our clothes, the point of contact between us and the world, especially other people. It is an interface that should be looked after and kept in good order. Just as we care for our body's cleanliness and good health, and just as we care that our clothes are clean and do not offend others or leave a bad impression, so too should we regard manners as something requiring regular attention and maintenance. In Islam, manners are not a superficial polish, nor a specialized routine for special occasions, nor a preserve of the upper classes. Rather, the same manners are recommended for all Muslims, of high or low status, rich or poor, and for all occasions.

The basic rules are (1) that we strive to do no harm by the way we speak or eat or dress or do any business in the world, and (2) that we strive to do some good by the way we speak or eat or dress or do any business in the world. In both cases, sincerity is a requirement. In fact, since insincerity is a type of doing harm, it is safest to avoid it by striving not to be too fussy, too pleasing, or too charming, but to keep things at a steady, simple level, which can be sustained, and which can be the same for most situations. You may ask: how can we know what this steady level is?

There is no rigid definition. It is relative to time and place and occasion. Nevertheless, we can apply a couple of test questions that, I find, always give a pretty good indication of what the level should be. First, I ask: am I behaving like this—dressing like this or speaking like this, etc.—because that is what the situation requires or just in order to impress? Second, I ask: am I behaving like this because I consider myself to be strong or weak in relation to the other person? Doing things just to impress other people is a tremendous drain on resources—time, energy and wealth—and most of the time it can be avoided. It cannot always be avoided, unfortunately. Under the rule of doing no harm, sometimes we have to go along with the manners of others, in order not to offend—but in these cases, we can keep our involvement to a minimum (I am thinking of elaborate weddings and expensive banquets). More serious is the issue of disparities in power: to behave differently just because someone is weaker or stronger than ourselves implies a weak understanding of our equality of being creatures of the same One and only Creator. Any position of superiority with respect to someone else is in reality an added burden of responsibility and should be considered as a moral test. Most of the time, we fail this test. We behave too timidly before social superiors and fail to correct or challenge them when they are doing wrong—of course there are rules within Islamic manners on how to correct or challenge social superiors. On the other side, we behave too impatiently or unkindly to social inferiors, and fail to take sufficient account of their independent right to have their opinion, or their tastes, or their needs, just as we like to have ours.

Behind these failures in manners is a failure to understand correctly what is due from us to our Creator. I try to imagine myself in the situation of the Prophet Yūsuf, alone in the well, with no-one to rely on except God. How he thinks and speaks then is how we should hope to maintain our good manners in relation to God. I try to imagine myself in his situation of powerlessness among strangers in a strange land, the temptation presented to him, and how he survived that, and how he behaved with his fellow-prisoners and then with the king. Precisely because he had a strong, clear hold on his duty to his Creator, his manners and decisions are consistently impeccable, consistently wise, and, eventually, lead to the best outcome. Clarity and strength in our manners with respect to God is the only secure means, through the diverse trials of life, of inclining to forgive others and deserving forgiveness ourselves. Being inclined to forgive the mistakes of others, while constantly alert to our own need to be forgiven for our mistakes, is the heart of good manners: without that heart, manners degenerate into routines and artifice, like surface polish, or a burden.

7

WHO TAUGHT YOU TO REMEMBER GOD

They asked: We always hear you reminding us of our Lord, reminding us to glorify Him, praise Him, seek refuge in Him, and to seek His aid. You encourage and inspire us to love Him, to obey Him, and to worship Him. How do we train ourselves to develop this connection with God and cultivate it further?

I replied: God is our Lord and our Master—and there is no Lord nor Master other than He. Remembering Him is our reliance, His praise our nourishment, and His glorification our provision. With His love, life becomes sweet and pleasant, and without it, bitter and unpleasant. When He is pleased with us it matters not if the rest of creation is angry. When the bond between us and Him is strong, it does not matter if that which is between us and the world is broken. To Him we continually submit until we earn His good pleasure.

There is no way for us to strengthen our connection with Him other than remembering Him profusely, morning and evening, and seeking from Him all assistance and refuge. We ask Him alone and fortify ourselves with Him alone. We become indifferent to all other than Him and turn to Him alone.

They asked: What will help us in this regard, for our desires and laziness have overwhelmed us?

I replied: You need to tenaciously hold on to two characteristics:

1. Reciting the Qur'ān with deliberation and understanding, casting your sharp eye deep into its apparent and inner meanings.
2. Keeping the company of the pious ones who are humble and obedient, for such company has an amazing effect on cleansing the soul, rectifying hearts, connecting them with God and orienting them to the discovery of and intense longing for God.

They asked: Can you mention some of the pious ones whom you accompanied, benefiting from them by remembering God and seeking access to Him in humility and repentance?

Biography of Muḥammad Aḥmad of Pratapgarh

I replied: There are over ten such individuals, but the most excellent of them and the most solid in rank and honor is the preeminent and unique Mawlānā Muḥammad Aḥmad of Pratapgarh, God the Exalted have mercy on him.

They asked: Please give us a glimpse into his life to familiarize us with him. I replied: He is the godly and pious scholar, fearful and pure, Muḥammad Aḥmad son of Ghulām Muḥammad from Pratapgarh, born in the year 1317/1899 in Pālpūr in the district of Pratapgarh. He learned from the great scholar and ḥadīth expert, the memorizer of Ṣaḥīḥ Bukhārī, Badr ʻAlī from Sadūnah in Raebareli, one of the spiritual successors of Faḍl al-Raḥmān Ganjmurādābādī. From Badr ʻAlī he received Ijāzah and successorship in the spiritual path.[53] He then met Mawlānā Wārith Ḥasan al-Ḥusaynī the Ḥanafī scholar of Kūra, Lucknow and one of the spiritual successors of the scholar of India Maḥmūd al-Ḥasan of Deoband. Under his leadership and training, he underwent difficult exercises and prolonged struggles in the historic and famous Mosque of the Mound in Lucknow.[54]

He then undertook the path of calling others to God, turning himself away from worldly connections and curbing the soul's stubbornness in the face of worldly interests. He traveled through towns and villages to teach people their religion, and to reform, purify, and train them. He did so with no regard for food, drink, clothing or shelter, and adopted as his path the love of God, preferring Him to all else and forsaking the world. In the end, he settled in the city of Allahabad where people from all over the land sought him out. He became a refuge and reference point for people. I have seen the greatest scholars of our time—like our Shaykh Abū al-Ḥasan ʻAlī Nadwī, the great ḥadīth scholar Ḥabīb al-Raḥmān Aʻẓamī, the Godly scholar Abrār al-Ḥaqq, and the reciter Ṣiddīq Aḥmad Bāndawī—prefer him over themselves, visit him frequently and drink from his pure and fresh spring. He faithfully persisted on this path until his worldly term came to an end on Sunday, the 3rd of Rabīʻ al-Thānī of 1412/1991 in the city of Allahabad at over ninety years

---

[53] In the spiritual hierarchy and practice of Sufi orders, a spiritual master (shaykh) would take a pledge of allegiance (bayʻah) from each follower (murīd) for their spiritual path or journey. From these followers, the master would deputize some of those who were competent enough to become his successors (khalīfah).

[54] The Tīlī Wālī Masjid, named after the mound (tīla) upon which it stands, is a historic 350-year mosque built by the Mughal ruler Aurangzeb that houses 6,000 worshippers and is an exquisite example of Mughal architecture.

of age. He left behind many children, including Mawlānā Ishtiyāq Aḥmad, Irshād Aḥmad and the reciter Mushtāq Aḥmad.

They asked: Tell us about his virtues. I replied: He was without equal in the qualities of worship, love of God, annihilation in His presence, complete reliance upon Him, abstinence from the world, contentment and humility. He was pure without being sullied in the least, and faithfully kept his secret with God.[55] He abundantly recited the Qur'ān with deliberation and contemplation, and adopted the manners and characteristics of the Prophet, peace be upon him. His words had great influence over hearts and command over people. Scholars, pious individuals and common people—even Hindus—were attracted to him in an amazing way, humbled by his love, appreciation, reverence, and veneration. Our Shaykh Abū al-Ḥasan ʿAlī Nadwī, God have mercy on him, said: "From the very first time that I visited him, I found him to be extremely simple in his dress and language. I found no trace of fame in him at all. When I heard his exhortations, I found in them such sincerity, spirituality, Godliness, remembrance of God, reminders of the Hereafter, turning to God and reforming the souls, which are rarely found among preachers and speakers."

They asked: Tell us about your connection to him. I replied: I visited him on more than one occasion with my companions in Lucknow and Allahabad. He might well be the best of the pious and Godly scholars that I sat with and accompanied. Whenever we visited him, he embraced us and brought us close to him, hugging us tightly with a heart full of love and tenderness. In this he was like a loving mother or a tender father. This was his practice with all those who came to him, and this love came naturally to him without being forced. I used to be amazed by his resolve, energy, strength and speed despite his advanced age and frail body. He always advised us to recite the Noble Qur'ān and follow the sunnah. I never saw him except that I was immediately reminded of God. He was extremely humble and always sat with his visitors, sharing food and drink with them and expressing concern for their affairs. He always advised them with whatever came to him from inspiration. He did not save any wealth nor acquire a single coin, despite the opening of the world to him towards the last days of his life.

---

[55] Keeping one's secret in the spiritual terminology of taṣawwuf refers to not divulging the intimacy and closeness one enjoys privately with God.

They asked: Did you seek ijāzah from him? I replied: Unfortunately, I was deprived of his ijāzah. Had I requested him, he would surely have obliged me. His isnād (chain) was extremely rare and elevated,[56] for he narrated from his teacher in knowledge and the spiritual path, the great ḥadīth scholar Badr 'Alī who narrated from the great muḥaddīth and Godly scholar Faḍl al-Raḥmān Ganjmurādābādī.

They asked: Why are you regretful over losing this ijāzah, for you have attained ijāzah from so many others who are also students of Faḍl al-Raḥmān Ganjmurādābādī? I replied: You are right, but his was a rare chain: the narration of a great ḥadīth scholar and shaykh of the spiritual path who narrates from his like who narrates from his like—and the three of them are known for knowledge, reform, teaching and training. And then there is a degree of elevation and rarity in the chain as well. I surely love Maulānā Muḥammad Aḥmad greatly, hold him in high esteem, and wish that I would have sought his ijāzah to have the honor of narrating from him.

They asked: What was the extent of his love for God and his remembrance of Him? I replied: He was overtaken by love, such that he and love became like two necessary twins, troubling the heart with perpetual torment and with a fire continuing to inflame without fully destroying. He stood on the path of the beloved, attaching his heart to Him, and finding comfort in His presence and company.

They asked: Tell us about his poetry. I replied: He was a gifted poet. Love pervaded his poetry. In that, he would become ecstatic and carried away, until utilizing his natural disposition and skill to compose verses filled with academic points, admonitions, faith-filled emotions, and religious zeal. His poetry was published in a work called *'Urfān-e-maḥabbat,* which contained a foreword from our Shaykh Abū al-Ḥasan 'Alī Nadwī. I also translated a small poem of his from Urdu into Arabic, which was published in a newsletter in Nadwah. He was extremely happy about that and supplicated for me in a letter he wrote to me, which tragically I have lost.

In his poetry, he spoke about the extent of his love:

Love's fire did burn me, causing me to perish
But in this demise, new life I have found

---

[56] An elevated chain is one with the fewest intermediaries to the source of the narration. The fewer the intermediaries, the higher—and more virtuous—the chain.

However, he did not exceed any bounds in that love but placed the sharīʿah and intellect as a protector over it:

No trace of excess or failing has remained here now
For balance is found once real love is complete.

8

WHO TAUGHT YOU TO FEAR GOD

They asked: What is fear (khawf)? I replied: It is the fear of God—specifically, fear of His wrath and anger in this life and the next, the fear of standing before Him, and the fear of His Fire.

They asked: Why do we fear God when he is Most Kind and Compassionate, even more than our own mothers? I replied: Would you be happy disobeying your mothers and be deprived of their love, affection, tenderness and mercy? They replied: Of course not. I said: So fear of God is the fear of disobeying Him and being thus deprived of His love, affection, tenderness and mercy.

They asked: Is not our Lord ever-forgiving of our sins and ever-accepting of repentance? If we seek His forgiveness, He forgives us, and if we repent to Him, He readily accepts it. So why do you warn us in this way? I replied: The sincere servant, when he disobeys his Lord is ashamed to face him, even if he was graced with the Lord's pardon and forgiveness. Aswad b Yazīd used to strive greatly in his worship, even fasting to the point of harming his body. 'Alqamah b. Qays once asked him, "Why do you harm this body of yours?" He replied, "It is the comfort of my body that I am seeking." When he was dying, he began to weep. It was said to him, "Why all this sorrow?" He replied, "Why shouldn't I weep? What is more appropriate for me than that? By God, if I were given complete forgiveness from God, I would still be bothered by my great shame before Him for all that I did. Some people might have tiny sins which are forgiven, but the shame remains.[57]

They asked: What would help us increase this fear within us? I replied: Remembering death, for it is the greatest means and strongest motive to develop indifference to this world and desire for the next. It is surely a destroyer of all pleasures and an exposer of all heedlessness. Qatādah relates that Muṭarrif once said, "This death has ruined enjoyment for all pleasure-seekers, so seek that enjoyment which does not have any death after it."[58]

---

[57] Abū Na'īm, *Ḥilyat al-Awliyā'*.
[58] *Ibid.*

Remembering death is reforming the heart, while forgetting it leads to the heart's destruction. Sa'īd b. Jubayr said, "If the reminder of death were to leave my heart and mind, I fear that my heart would destroy me immediately."[59] Read my previous article on death and you will be shaken and experience some of this urgency.

They asked: From whom have you learned this type of fear? I replied: I am the furthest of people from possessing this type of fear. Had I really possessed it, my life would be far different. I would not have persisted in this heedlessness and falsehood of mine, and my sins would not have followed one after the other. I have dyed the tinges of the hair on my head with these vicissitudes of time and circumstance. However, I love dearly the ones who really possess this type of fear. I enjoy learning about their noble states and their wonderful stories, hoping that God would grant me a portion of that fear through their blessings.

They asked: What is your role model in this fear? I replied: The model for all people in fear and all other virtues are the Prophets and Messengers of God, followed by the Companions and then all pious and chosen individuals. But I will select for you one example that caught my heart and seized my soul, a model that I became fascinated with and desirous of.

The Exemplary Fear of Sufyān al-Thawrī

They asked: Who is that? I replied: He is the Imām, jurist, and abstinent one Sufyān b. Sa'īd b. Masrūq al-Thawrī (d. 161/778), who was a leading figure in this type of fear.

They said: Tell us some of those features of his. I replied: I will share what Dhahabī said in his biographical entry in *Siyar a'lām al-nubalā'*:

> Yūsuf b. Asbāṭ said: "When Sufyān used to be seized by the reminder of the next life, he would experience bleeding in his urine." 'Abd al-Raḥmān b. Mahdī said: "Sufyān came to us while we used to sleep most of the night. When he began to stay with us, we used to sleep far less." He also said: "Sufyān used to shout when his illness became prolonged, 'O death! O death!' He then would follow-up by saying, 'We don't wish for

[59] *Ibid.*

> it, nor do we ask for it.' When he was on his deathbed, he began to weep and become fearful. I said to him, 'Abū 'Abdullah, why do you weep?' He replied, "Abd al-Raḥmān, because of the intensity of my experience with death. Death is so hard!' I touched him and he was saying, 'The soul of the believer leaves like perspiration. I hope for that!' He then reminded himself, 'God is more merciful than a tender, loving mother. He is most Generous and Bountiful. How can I love to meet Him, while I hate death?' I myself began to weep until I began to choke, trying to hide my crying from him. He then began to cry out, 'Oh! Oh!' from the pangs of death."
>
> Yaḥyā b. Yamān relates from Sufyān that he said, "Had animals understood death the way you do, you would not eat from them to your fill." Then Yaḥyā said: "I have not seen the likes of Sufyān. The world was presented to him, and he turned his face from it." 'Abd al-Raḥmān Rustah said: "Sufyān stayed with me once and began to cry. He was asked why, and responded, 'Because I belittle my sins to less than this—and he raised up something from the ground—and I fear losing my faith prior to dying.'" 'Abd al-Raḥmān b. Mahdī said: "Sufyān suffered from an ailment of the stomach. One night, he performed ablution sixty times, until he realized the matter, came off his bed and put his cheek to the ground, saying: "Abd al-Raḥmān, how tough is death!'"[60]

They said: We wish we had a portion of this fear. I replied: Let us pray to God that he distribute portions of this fear among us that would stop us from our disobedience and help us firmly fight our temptations. Desires can be so stubborn and overpowering.

They asked: Were there any one of your teachers that had this type of fear, surpassing his peers? I replied: There were many teachers who feared God in this way, but I could not focus on this aspect of their lives.

They said: You have accompanied such a large number of teachers, taking from them arts and sciences and etiquette. How could the likes of you be so careless and negligent?

---

[60] Dhahabī, *Siyar a'lām al-nubalā'*.

A Fearful Companion of Mine

I replied: I have often wondered the same. However, I did meet a young and pious scholar in the city of the Prophet, peace be upon him, one whom I think did have a portion of this type of fear. His love arose in my heart. Every time I saw him or reviewed my encounters with him, it would reinforce this notion in my heart that he feared God.

They said: You have enticed our curiosity, so who is he? I replied: I fear mentioning his name, lest he become angry with me and cut off the bond, connection and closeness we share.

They said: You speak to us about the fear of God, and you fear other than Him? I replied: I fear God, but I also fear those that fear God.

They asked: We have seen you criticizing those who say that they fear God and also fear those who do not fear God. Is that not the same as your statement? I replied: The one who fears those who have no fear of God has adopted an evil and wicked stance that is to be rejected. God says in His Book, *"It was Satan who suggested to you the fear of his allies. Do not fear them, but fear Me, if you truly believe."*[61] As for fearing those who fear God, however, then that is the fear of the allies of the Merciful One. When they get angry, God gets angry. Any fear that stems from the fear of God or leads to the fear of God is praiseworthy, like the fear of death, fear of the Day of Judgment, or fear of the Fire.

They said: We wish you would name him to us, so that we may visit him and learn from his life. I replied: What prevents me from that is the fear of unjustifiably claiming someone is purified, or that I may be a reason for his trial, for the living are not immune from trials. The man has benefited me through his companionship, and it pains me that I might reward him with evil.

They replied: Please describe him to us. I replied: Descriptions are a substitute for naming, but I will mention to you some of his positions which may benefit you. I saw him once attend a scholarly assembly where people began mentioning various scholars which led to some argument. He became angry with them and firmly rejected what they were doing, without concern for their status or their friendship. I have also seen him reading Ṣaḥīḥ Bukhārī to some teachers where matters escalated to involving excessive criticism of some religious organizations, which led to considering their right positions

[61] Qur'ān 3:175.

wrong while ignoring the mistakes of their opponents. He rose up with great passion and, motivated by loyalty to God alone, defended the truth in a firm way. I have found him to be the farthest of people from arguing with others, and one who detested enjoying the flesh of scholars.[62] May God reward him for his honesty and multiply those rewards abundantly.

They said: Tell us more. I replied: Read the Book of God and pay attention to the lives of the Prophets and righteous individuals. Perhaps God would grant you His fear through that. And strive to realize this fear within yourselves, for it is a light that would illuminate darkness for you. It awakens individuals while the rest of people sleep in their heedlessness. It represents salvation for the seekers and for the righteous. What an excellent thing Shaykh al-Islām Ibn Taymiyyah said: "The root of all good in this life and the next is the fear of God."[63]

---

[62] Allusion to back-biting.
[63] Ibn Taymiyyah. *Majmū' al-Fatāwā.*

9

WHO TAUGHT YOU GENEROSITY OF SPIRIT

They asked: What is the meaning of generosity of spirit (samāḥah)? I replied: It means to be easy, gentle, generous and benevolent. It is a pure and noble human character trait which inclines one to become affable to others and facilitating of their affairs. It also inspires one to respect and do good to others. The generous-hearted person is pleasant, gentle and kind, profusely generous, having good thoughts of others and overlooking of their mistakes. He finds excuses for others and is always pleased with them. He is never stubborn or harsh, nor rough or rude. He is jubilant and cheerful with others, and never frowning or somber in their faces.

They asked: We find in you signs and characteristics of this generosity of spirit, which is rare in others. I replied: I am not generous of heart by nature or temperament, but I have adopted it by stealing it from some of my teachers.

Generosity of Abū al-Ḥasan ʿAlī Nadwī

They asked: Who taught you this generosity of spirit from your many teachers possessing differing temperaments? I replied: People are so far removed from this generosity of spirit and it evades most of them. Perhaps the best of my teachers in this trait was the great leader and noble scholar Abū al-Ḥasan ʿAlī Nadwī. He was like abundant rain, noble and earnest, with lovely character traits like pure gold. He was far above being difficult with others. I have seen many individuals after him, but never found any one who could match his generosity of heart. He was a man who lived his life having completely perfected this trait. There are many living ones among us who have been dead for a long time, but I speak of him as if he were still alive among us. I continue to see his guidance, manners and habits. I can see the heavenly glimpses on his face, and the pure, angelic imprints on his heart, which would illuminate assemblies and gatherings with great dignity and serenity.

They said: Describe for us some glimpses of his generosity so that we emulate those and take them as guides. I replied: I will describe four aspects of his generosity:

First, he possessed great generosity of spirit with respect to differing views and schools of thought. He was raised in a time where every person reveled in his own views and was a partisan of his own school while casting arrows of censure, slander and insult at others. People harbored rancor, jealousy and hatred against one another. Shaykh Abū al-Ḥasan lived estranged from these people of his time, far above them with his pure heart and sound motives. He was respectful of others and treated them with honor. He never looked at their affiliations, and always sought to reconcile people and mend hearts. He brought together scholars and leaders, highlighting their virtues and accomplishments while minimizing their shortcomings and defects. He avoided exposing what would harm others or bring out their secrets. He despised differing and fighting. He was protected from enmity and hatred, and avoided refuting and arguing.

Second, he had the greatest love for his associates and students. He was extremely close to all of his associates and students, full of tender love and affection. He would come to them faithfully, overlook their mistakes and dismiss their lapses. He shared in their discussions, and in their joys and sorrows. He would joke with them tenderly and thereby lighten some of their burdens. His gatherings were those of knowledge and respect, history and biographies. There was no belittling nor disregard for anyone. No one would be faulted or exposed. There was no mockery or loud laughter in his assemblies, no artificial displays or false pretenses, and no flattery. He honored all attendees, even when they were absent. He preserved others' secrets, never offending them or talking about them in their absence. He could not imagine harming anyone or harboring against them any rancor or malice, not to mention resentment or irritation. He was the freest of people from any envy, quarrel or evil trait. He was devoid of grievance for injury and avoided quarreling with others. He resisted all sins and abominations with his hearing, sight and tongue.

Third, he would always prefer others when he sensed a need to answer a question, issue a ruling, or offer an opinion. People of knowledge and understanding find it heavy to make a display of their knowledge or boast about their views or opinions, or to rush into that which they are not proficient in. In that, he was a replica of the predecessors in protecting himself from speaking on matters his peers could suffice. Ibn Abī Laylah states: "I have met one hundred and twenty Companions of the Anṣār, and whenever anyone of them were asked about something, they would endeavor to refer the question to one other, until it often returned back to them after the rest also declined to answer. Whenever they spoke on a matter or asked a question, they would always prefer their brothers in their place." I accompanied Shaykh Abū al-Ḥasan on an academic trip to Samarqand and Bukhārā which included a group of scholars including Shaykh 'Abd al-Fattāḥ Abū Ghuddah. I found these two shaykhs reciprocating respect and honor for one another. While returning to Samarqand from Bukhārā, the time for Maghrib approached and it was difficult to perform ablution or to pray. We did not know what to do, so I asked Shaykh Abū al-Ḥasan. He ordered me to ask Shaykh 'Abd al-Fattāḥ, who replied, "We shall pray Maghrib and 'Ishā' in a combined manner in our hotel in Samarqand." Shaykh Abū al-Ḥasan readily accepted this answer and was fully satisfied.[64]

Fourth, he had tremendous generosity as a host. All sorts of people would visit Shaykh Abū al-Ḥasan, from his friends and associates to strangers, including both men and women. He would welcome them heartily, extending to all his wonderful manner and affection. His hands were open and his grace immense, without any sense of indebtedness. He was never annoyed or harsh. He never extended insult to anyone nor withheld any good. If there were anyone bent upon hating him, he would be patient and not return the offense, pardoning them instead. He fully recognized the rights of people—and only truly noble individuals fully recognize the rights of people. Those with needs returned from him fully quenched and satisfied.

They said: Tell us more about his generosity. It is so pleasant that it makes the hearts soft. I replied: We will stop with this amount, for remembering him beckons my heart and gives me great pain. Have mercy on me, if you are of those who have mercy on your teachers. May my soul be ransomed for Shaykh Abū al-Ḥasan, the teacher and advisor that rendered me free from all other teachers and advisers, the one whose virtues I never cease to praise. God reward him with that which my thanks or tongue could

---

[64] It should be noted that in the Ḥanafī jurisprudential school as followed by most Indian scholars, the five prayers are performed separately in their own times, even while traveling. For most other schools, including the practice of Ḥanafīs outside of the Indian subcontinent (as was the case of Shaykh 'Abd al-Fattāḥ), travel serves as a hardship exemption which allows one to combine their prayers.

never do justice. Were it not for him, I would not have met those above me or preferred over myself those lesser than me.

They said: What would you advise us? I replied: I advise you and myself to reflect on his life and the lives of the righteous, pious, God-fearing and chosen ones before him. Strive to acquire this generosity of spirit, seeking it out actively and learning to love it. Brothers are many but the trustworthy ones are few. Do not tarnish your character with any evil. Be people of leniency, ease and generosity. Do not argue or utter any falsehood. The character of those who are generous-hearted is known by striving for beauty and refraining from harm, and avoiding those who betray friendship and affection.

◈10◈

WHO TAUGHT YOU GENTLENESS

They said: What is the meaning of gentleness (rifq)? I replied: Gentleness is to soften your tone in speech and action and to exhibit amiable behavior and civility in interaction. It is the companion of prudence and circumspection,[65] and its opposite is offense and harshness. Gentleness has the delicate quality of flowing water, as it enters into persons readily and diffusely, without any force or difficulty. Gentleness is the most successful path, while harshness is the worst. Gentleness eases those things that are considered difficult, while harshness makes all things more difficult.

They said: We are being tried by the rise of harshness and severity among people in general, and even among scholars, teachers and leaders. I replied: You are right. Nothing pains me more than seeing scholars treating each other harshly or sternly, even to the point of reviling and cursing. Such individuals violate the norms of conduct by placing harshness and severity in the place of gentleness and mercy. They go to excesses in their zeal and emotion, defiantly using their tongues for abuse and their actions for oppression. They become a blemish and disgrace to knowledge and its practitioners, and a shame and disgrace to wisdom and its adherents.

They said: Tell us more about the true role of gentleness and its importance so that we may plant its roots and pillars within and around ourselves. I replied: God encouraged it in His Book and raised its status when He said to Mūsā and his brother Hārūn, *"Go both of you to Pharaoh, for he has transgressed all bounds, and speak to him gently, perhaps he may take heed or become apprehensive."*[66] He also said to our Prophet, peace be upon him, *"And lower your wing to those who follow you of the believers."*[67] He said while praising the Prophet, *"It was thanks to God's mercy that you were gentle to them. Had you been rough, hard-hearted, they would surely have*

---

[65] Careful deliberation and examination, as opposed to hastily rushing to words and statements that may potentially offend.

[66] Qur'ān 20:43-4.

[67] Qur'ān 26:215.

scattered away from you."[68] Muslim relates from Jarīr that the Prophet, peace be upon him, said, "He who is deprived of gentleness is deprived of all good."[69] Muslim also relates from ʿĀ'ishah who said: I heard the Prophet, peace be upon him, say while he was in my house: "O God, whoever acquires some kind of control over the affairs of my people and is hard upon them, be You hard upon him, and whoever acquires some kind of control over the affairs of my people and is kind to them, be Thou kind to him."[70]

Biography of ʿAbd al-Fattāḥ Abū Ghuddah

They said: The Qur'ān and Sunnah are very clear concerning its danger and its virtue, and it pleases us that we see a portion of this noble trait within you. Who have you taken as a role model in this? I replied: He was our teacher, the noble ḥadīth scholar and expert, the great jurist, Shaykh ʿAbd al-Fattāḥ Abū Ghuddah. He had a beautiful face and smiling countenance. He stood tall with a dignified and noble appearance. He had a graceful aura, beautiful clothes and a pleasant aroma. He exhibited Prophetic character traits. He was quick to tears, weeping at the recitation of the Qur'ān and reminders of the predecessors. I asked him to say some words while we were at the tomb of Imām Bukhārī in Hartang in Samarqand. He issued some moving reminders, which made him cry as well as those around him. The great scholar Saʿīd Ḥawwā remarked, "I've never seen or met a scholar about whom this verse was more applicable—'*They were such that when the words of the Most Compassionate Lord were recited to them, they fell down in prostration, weeping.*'[71]—than our shaykh Muḥammad al-Ḥāmid and our shaykh ʿAbd al-Fattāḥ Abū Ghuddah."

I also said: God blessed me to learn about this shaykh and connect with him. I benefited from his knowledge as well as his character. Perhaps what pleased me the most about him was his gentleness and his prudence in affairs. He took gentleness as his permanent companion, and it was with him wherever he went. When he left a place, it would become devoid of gentleness and prudence.

---

[68] Qur'ān 3:159.

[69] Ṣaḥīḥ Muslim: Kitāb al-birr wa al-ṣilah wa al-ādāb. Bāb faḍl al-rifq.

[70] Ṣaḥīḥ Muslim: Kitāb al-imārah. Bāb faḍīlat al-imām al-ʿādil wa ʿuqūbat al-jā'ir wa al-ḥathth ʿalā al-rifq ʿan al-raʿiyyah wa al-nahy ʿan idkhāl al-mashaqqah ʿalayhim.

[71] Qur'ān 19:58.

They said: Tell us some aspects of his gentleness. I replied: I will summarize it in five points:

First, there was his gentleness in speech: He was extremely sweet in his speech, pleasant in his logic and elegant in his expressions. He was ever close to the hearts of his audience, capturing them with his pleasant words and pleasing them with his flowing expression and smooth tongue. When he spoke, he weighed every word, and they flowed like honey. Listeners would enjoy them and want more. He was not one to chatter or talk inconsequentially, which only serves to expose flaws and errors.

Second, his gentleness in conduct: He was extremely refined in his conduct, in public and private. He was gentle in his mannerisms and all customs and habits, from dress, food, and drink, to the arrangement of his works, the way he dealt with pages, pens and books, and his manner of authorship and writing.

Third, his gentleness in his teaching: When teaching is marked by softness and calmness of voice, it is far more influential and effective and far more likely to be accepted. On the other hand, a loud and harsh voice incites opposition and disagreement. Our shaykh owned the hearts of his students. They loved him as they came under the influence of his gentleness and good conduct.

Some students opposed his views. It was revealed to me that he used to refer to the city of the Prophet as *al-Madīnah al-Munawwarah* ('radiant city') while teaching in some universities. On one instance, a student intending to stir up trouble stood up and shouted, "And why is it radiant?" He must have supposed that he would answer, "By the grave of the Prophet," to which he would then respond. But the shaykh answered with great gentleness and calm, "It is radiant by the descent of revelation." The student was silenced, and he returned to his seat.

Fourth, his gentleness in dealing with others: He was cordial and loving in his dealings with others. He was always lenient towards people and never stubborn, and always modest and noble. He was polite with others and always flattered them sincerely. He never offended or insulted anyone. He was elegant and light-hearted, and joked with his audience to appropriate extents. He did not burden them with anything they found difficult. When any negativity arose suddenly from the audience against him which did not suit his position, he ignored it out of noble kind-heartedness.

Fifth, his gentleness with his opponents: He was forbearing and frequent to forgive and pardon. He protected himself from being soiled by insults or other bad traits. He attained by his gentleness what others could not. Hearts and souls were attracted to him and loved him. He was the target of evil and ugly words which should have no place in the discourse of scholars. In spite of that, he was patient and persistent in his kindness, like a mountain unswayed by heavy winds. The foolish, on the other hand, are like flickering flames which are put out by the slightest wind. Once he mentioned some of these detractors to me, without naming them, while shyness was brimming from his face. He was applying the ḥadīth that was related by Bukhārī from ʿĀʾishah that some Jewish persons had come to the Prophet and greeted him with, *al-sāmu ʿalaykum* ("may you be poisoned"). ʿĀʾishah responded to them, "And upon you too, may God curse you and rain down His wrath upon you!" The Prophet said to her, "Easy, ʿĀʾishah! Be kind and beware of harshness and bad words."[72]

I also said: And it was God's mercy upon the shaykh through the grace of his kindness and good conduct that his praises lived on and his name continues to be mentioned with pride and honor, while the words of his detractors have dissipated like dust.

They said: Our hearts have become filled with love and respect for your teacher. I replied: He was truly worthy of receiving love, honor and great respect.

Training Yourselves to Be Kind

They asked: How do we train ourselves in this type of kindness? I replied: Virtues are not amassed except through great effort and struggle. So fight against your desires and your inner selves. Subdue them with gentleness and softness of speech and conduct. In gentleness lies good fortune and success, while in offending is harshness and error that ultimately leads to failure. If people were armed with every type of weapon to fulfill their need, it would not be fulfilled except by the one who possesses this quality. When you are faced with harm, proceed with deliberation and know that gentleness is a trait of those who are skillful and resourceful.

[72] Ṣaḥīḥ Bukhārī: Kitāb al-adab. Bāb lam yakun al-nabiyy fāḥishan wa lā mutafaḥḥishan.

Remember what Muslim relates from 'Ā'ishah that the Prophet, peace be upon him, said: "Gentleness is not to be found in anything except that it adorns it, and is not withdrawn from anything except that it tarnishes it."[73]

[73] Ṣaḥīḥ Muslim: Kitāb al-birr wa al-ṣilah wa al-ādāb. Bāb faḍl al-rifq.

11

WHO TAUGHT YOU FORBEARANCE

They asked: What is the meaning of forbearance (ḥilm)? I replied: It is to be calm, composed and restrained in the face of anger or provocation, and to refrain from cursing those who are immoral or reacting against those who are dishonorable and offensive. Forbearance, despite the capacity to respond, is a major part of generosity and benevolence. The destiny and outcome of forbearance is nothing but good. It is a treasure that isn't lost while expending it, and a shade and refuge that manifests the attribute of the Ever-Merciful One. It is the purest of traits of the Prophets, Messengers and pious ones. It is a shield from the plots of the devil and protection from the attacks of one's base self, from the heedlessness of the frivolous, and from the carelessness of the ignorant.

They said: God described Ismāʿīl as forbearing *("We gave him (Ibrāhīm) the good news of a forbearing child")*[74] and steadfast (*"And (We bestowed the same favor) upon Ismāʿīl, Idrīs and Dhu al-Kifl, for they were all steadfast."*).[75] He also quoted him as saying, *"You shall find me, if God so wills, from the steadfast."*[76] Do forbearance and patience/steadfastness go hand in hand? I replied: They are not synonymous with one another, but they are inseparable. Patience (ṣabr) means holding back or restraining oneself, and is of three types:

1. Holding back from disobedience
2. Persisting in obedience (i.e. holding back from abandoning them)
3. Patience/restraint in the face of adversity and difficulty (i.e holding back from despair, bad thoughts, giving up, etc.)

So Ismāʿīl was forbearing and, at the same time, steadfast—two conforming and symmetrical qualities. He exhibited extreme patience in his

---

[74] Qur'ān 37:101.
[75] Qur'ān 21:85.
[76] Qur'ān 37:102.

readiness to be sacrificed out of obedience and submission to God. This was a level of patience that could not hope to be achieved by most determined people, not even the mightiest mountains. What supreme steadfastness that was, without the slightest care or worry, and what sublime submission and obedience! His forbearance was his calculated perseverance at a moment where even the most composed and poised individuals would have failed. How can a person be composed when his father would say to him, *"My son, I see in my dream that I am slaughtering you"*?[77] These words are surely capable of provoking even the calmest people, depriving them of the realization of righteousness and obedience while provoking rebellion and disobedience. Have the heavens and earth ever witnessed an illustration as radiant and lofty as his, or calmness as pure and virtuous as his?

They asked: Has anyone other than Ismāʿīl been described with this trait of forbearance in the Qur'ān? I replied: Yes. Who can forget Ibrāhīm, the beloved of God, the best of the world in forbearance and poise? How perfectly composed he was, and how completely calm and collected! When God sent the angels with the punishment to the people of Lūṭ, and they brought the good news to Ibrāhīm: *"He said: 'O Messengers, what is your errand?' They replied: 'Behold, we have been sent to a wicked people.'"*[78] He began to plead to his Lord to stop the punishment, or postpone it for a while. God says: *"Surely Ibrāhīm was forbearing, tenderhearted and oft-turning to God. [The angels said:] 'O Abraham, give up this [plea]. Indeed, the command of your Lord has come, and indeed, there will reach them a punishment that cannot be repelled.'"*[79] He exhibited supreme forbearance, composure and peace of mind and heart. Look at the tremendous difference and vast distance between his example and that of Muslims today. In our times, many are eager for immediate punishment for their enemies. They curse them and pray for their destruction. Lūṭ's people used to practice abominations and surely deserved punishment, but Ibrāhīm pleaded to his Lord, restraining himself from anger at a time that would incite even the most intelligent ones to fury and rage.

They said: We find in you the mark of forbearance, constancy of pressure and balanced views. You are not incited by resentment or anger as others are. I replied: I am not forbearing, but I try to practice forbearance, patience,

---

[77] Qur'ān 37:102.
[78] Qur'ān 51:31-2.
[79] Qur'ān 11:75-6.

composure and restraint. The fire of rage does ignite within me and threatens to dissipate all marks of forbearance, but then I quickly become regretful and repenting, and resolve to maintain forbearance. Thus, my life is a running struggle between forbearance and anger, whereas the best forbearance is that which is part of one's nature.

They asked: Who is your model for forbearance? I replied: My models are Ibrāhīm and Ismā'īl, as well as our Prophet Muḥammad, peace be upon him, Abū Bakr, Abū 'Ubaydah b. al-Jarrāḥ, and others from our predecessors.

Biography of Muḥammad Rābi' Ḥasanī Nadwī

They asked: Can you mention one of your teachers whom you have considered to be forbearing and from whom you have learned this trait in a practical way? I replied: He is our teacher, the eminent scholar and scion of Prophetic lineage, Muḥammad Rābi' Ḥasanī Nadwī. He was generous-natured and kind-hearted, and possessed a refined character and many valuable traits. He was the best person from whom I learned the traits of forbearance and patience.

They asked: Can you tell some of the signs of his forbearance? I replied: They are three:

First, there was his forbearance at the incitement of anger. I found him to the most perfect person in calmness and composure, for he would not be incited to anger or frustration by any of the usual things. I have never observed him, during the course of my studies at Nadwat al-'Ulamā', to ever become angry with us whatever the circumstances were. He was burdened with great administrative responsibilities at the institution. On many occasions, he would arrive late for our classes. We would take advantage of his tardiness by going to the cafeteria to get tea, and a student would come to call us back when he had arrived. We would return to find him sitting alone, and he would begin the class without expressing any iota of anger or dissatisfaction. Once he called us to his office to inform us that the designated course material had not been completed, due to mistakes on his part as well as ours. He did not blame us exclusively but shared in it. Once someone senior to him reviled him with ugly words, but he kept himself controlled from any outbursts, without any hint of anger or hostility.

Second, there was his forbearance during trying times where people would lose themselves to grudges, hatred and flared emotions. One of the ordeals we experienced in our time stemmed from the issue of the Bābrī Masjid in India.[80] His stance during these times was that of a composed and serious scholar, and that prevented him from acting out of haste or operating from chauvinism or emotions. He was steadfast in the face of that ordeal like a wise and intelligent person, with the interests of his ummah and nation at heart. Similarly, when the Persian Gulf War broke out and inflicted such a toll and destruction that only God is fully aware of, and when earthquakes and disasters came in quick succession and people witnessed signs of great tribulation and became agitated and unrestful in the Arab and Islamic world, we always found him calm and steadfast. He expended his efforts to quelling these ordeals, putting out these fires and calming the masses. He firmly set about taking every precaution to protect himself from these tribulations and ordeals.

Third, there was his forbearance in personal trials. He was extremely patient during personal offense and endured it calmly by restraining himself from expressing any anger or displeasure. He was not provoked by any malice and never allowed any hidden rancor to surface. He was of gentle disposition and lenient leadership. His colleagues always sought his company and enjoyed it, without ever becoming averse or bored, even in travel. One could consult him on any personal matter, and he would never rush. He would always advise in one's best interest. Those who are forbearing always advise in the best way, while the ignorant do the opposite. He would also frequently remain silent, and his deliberate silence was a part of his maturity and good sense in management and experience. On top of all of that, he had an aura of great respect. Whether he spoke or adopted silence, he did so not out of habit, but only to bring people to virtue and justice. Whenever we ignored his advice or views, we brought upon ourselves harm and adversity. This only made us love and respect his qualities of forbearance and patience even more. Indeed, the intelligent one through his calculated strategy can achieve that which kings with their steeds and soldiers cannot hope to achieve.

They asked: Have you ever seen him violate this trait and become regretful? I replied: No, we never saw in him any negligence or excess, or overstepping bounds, or the likes. Whereas many other leaders would energetically rush to action without adequate preparation and fall into lapses or expose themselves to errors—only to become regretful later—our shaykh

---

[80] The infamous destruction in 1992 of a 500-year-old mosque in Ayodhya by Hindu extremists that sparked communal violence across India.

was always calling to virtue and success, while avoiding evil and loss. He would not utter words except those he had pondered and deliberated. He would not speak about issues which did not concern him or about matters he was not asked about. He would never comment unless he was certain or had verified the matter. He left no room for regret or fear of adverse outcomes.

They asked: Can you name someone else from whom you learned forbearance? I replied: I will answer on condition that you not ask me about a third. They replied: Very well. I replied: He is our teacher Muḥammad Wāḍiḥ Rashīd Nadwī. They were so alike in their forbearance and patience, and their excellent example and lifestyle.

They asked: How would you advise us? I replied: I advise you and myself to practice restraint and never become a victim of your own anger. Do not burn others with your rage, for anger is the most hateful thing. Do not rush to adopt views, decisions or positions during times of trials and tribulations. Know that swimming with crocodiles is dangerous. Starve off hatred and malice from within yourselves and strip your heart from all resentments and ill-will. Be calm and composed, expending yourself only to please God. Know that deliberation, forbearance and composure is part of intelligence and honor. For the forbearing ones, there is tremendous virtue in their character. It is a cloak that never gets old and an aroma that never vanishes.

They said: Can you provide us with his biography? I replied: He is the eminent scholar, hailing from Prophetic lineage, the astute literary critic, the insightful one, Muḥammad Rābiʿ b. Rashīd Aḥmad b. Khalīl al-Dīn Aḥmad b. Rashīd al-Dīn b. Saʿīd al-Dīn Ṣābir b. Ghulām Jīlānī b. Muḥammad Wāḍiḥ b. Muḥammad Ṣābir b. Āyat Allāh b. ʿAlam Allāh al-Ḥasanī al-ʿAlawī. He was the son of the sister of our shaykh Abū al-Ḥasan ʿAlī Nadwī.

He was born in 1349/1929 in the neighborhood of the Godly scholar Mawlānā ʿAlam Allāh Barelvī, in one of the villages around Raebareli, eighty kilometers from Lucknow. He was raised in a well-known and honorable home known for purity, knowledge and practice. He completed all higher education at Nadwat al-ʿUlamā' and graduated in 1367/1947. He traveled to Saudi Arabia in 1371/1951, where he spent a year studying the sources of knowledge and literature, benefiting from many pious scholars, and visiting many libraries and other resources of knowledge. He specialized and excelled in Arabic literature, becoming well known in the discipline. He also specialized in the history of Arab nations and sociology, as well as the science of Qur'ānic exegesis and ḥadīth. He was blessed by God with receiving ijāzah from three senior individuals: Shaykh Abū al-Ḥasan 'Alī Nadwī, Mawlānā Muḥammad Zakariyyā Kāndihlawī and Shaykh 'Abd al-Fattāḥ Abū Ghuddah.

He became an assistant teacher in the College of Arabic at Nadwat al-'Ulamā' in the year 1368/1949 and became the head in 1382/1962. He then worked as the rector of Nadwat al-'Ulamā' from 1413/1992 until the death of Shaykh Abū al-Ḥasan, after which he succeeded his role as the leader of Nadwah.

He authored: *Qīmat al-ummah al-islāmiyyah wa munjizātuhā, Maqālāt fī al-tarbiyah wa al-mujtama', Manthūrāt fī adab al-'arab, al-Adab al-'arabī bayna 'arḍ wa naqd, Tārīkh al-adab al-'arabī, al-Adab al-islāmī wa ṣilatuhū bi al-ḥayāh, Mukhtār al-shi'r al-'arabī, al-'Ālam al-islāmī al-yawm, Rawā'i' min al-adab al-islāmī min al-qadīm, al-Muslimūn wa al-tarbiyah, Sirājan munīran, al-Dīn wa al-adab, Jazīrat al-'arab*, and many other valuable works in Arabic and Urdu, along with close to a hundred scholarly articles.

Our shaykh followed the way of the predecessors in his knowledge, practice, piety, caution, chastity, self-independence, abstinence, sincerity, forbearance, patience, balance, and moderation. I have been his companion for more than twenty years, and I have never seen any scholar or student of Nadwah—or for that matter, anyone outside of it—who was like him in that he was never the subject of any criticism in his practice or conduct.

I have had the honor of receiving numerous personal letters from him, most of them having to do with advice concerning my stay in Great Britain and my academic endeavors. I have heard from him the 'First Ḥadīth' (al-ḥadīth al-musalsal bi al-awwaliyyah)[81] in my home in Oxford on the 4th of Jamādī al-Ākhirah 1421/2000, and he granted me written ijāzah in it. I visited him in Takiyyat[82] Kulān in Raebareli in Ramadan 1433/2012 and performed i'tikāf[83] in the masjid along with him in the last ten days. I listened to his lectures, heard from him the musalsal ḥadīth narrations of al-awwaliyyah, al-

---

[81] The "musalsal" ḥadīth traditions are a genre of ḥadīth narrations that are patterned with a recurring story, a continuous action or other feature that consistently appears throughout its chain. In this case, al-ḥadīth al-musalsal bil-awwaliyyah ("the ḥadīth connected by being the first") is the first ḥadīth one hears from one's teacher, with this being the case at every, or most, links in the chain of narration.

[82] Takiyyah refers to a retreat built on the outskirts of towns by religious-minded individuals, much like a zāwiyah in various Muslim societies.

[83] The religious act of secluding oneself in the masjid in Ramadan for any number of days, preferably in the last ten.

muṣāfaḥah[84] and al-aswadayn.[85] I also read to him portions of his book *al-Adab al-'arabī bayna 'arḍ wa naqd,* hearing from him a commentary of each portion as well numerous beneficial academic and literary insights that you would be hard-pressed to find in any book. I also read to him the pre-Islamic mu'allaqāt odes of Imra' al-Qays and Ṭarafah b. al-'Abd. He also dictated to us his book *al-Tarbiyah wa al-mujtama',* in which he summarized ancient and contemporary societal views along with their practical implications in Islamic societies.

Our teacher was a great model for his students at Nadwat al-'Ulamā' in both academic and practical dimensions. Each student received his due share from his devotion and care, with genuine honor and beautiful humility. He only did so out of sincere empathy and affection, with the kindness of a father for his children.

---

[84] This is one of the musalsal ḥadīth narrations in which the student shakes the teacher's hand at every level of the chain.

[85] *Al-aswadayn* ("the two black things") is how Arabs referred to dates and water. In this musalsal ḥadīth, the teacher provides dates and water to the students at each level.

12

WHO TAUGHT YOU ISLAMIC THOUGHT

They asked: What exactly is Islamic thought? I replied: Islamic thought represents the sum of all intellectual feats in the sciences, arts, philosophy and literature that Muslims have collectively passed on to posterity in the spirit of innovation and invention, from the very beginning of Islam until today.

They asked: What is contemporary Islamic thought? I replied: It is pure and unblemished thinking advanced by Muslim thinkers to oppose secular constructs, to resist against Western intellectual and cultural attacks, and to correct revivalist thought unwittingly influenced by un-Islamic sources. It deals directly with studying the challenges and crises that face Muslims as a result of the Western military, political, intellectual and cultural invasion of the entire world; analyzing the effects of Western civilization and the resulting philosophies of evolution, existentialism, individualism, and the doctrines of secularism, democracy, and liberalism. All of these represent a stark challenge to Islamic thought, soil the purity of Islamic culture, contradict religious values and ethics oppose the highest human ideals, and cut off Muslims from their past and from their history.

They asked: What is the source of Islamic thought? I replied: Its source is the Noble Qur'ān and the Prophetic Sunnah, which must be approached in full detail and comprehension. From these sources, its details are derived and extracted, in which case it becomes Godly thought, meaning that it ultimately emanates from God and not from human beings. Consequently, it represents thought that is genuine and established, free from the influence of whims, desires, imported solutions and other defects.

They asked: What are its features? I replied: Islamic thought is distinguished by the loftiness and veracity of its sources. It is also comprehensive, in that it encompasses all the dictates and dimensions of life: from beliefs and conduct to social interaction, learning, economics and politics. It is a balanced and moderate approach, in that it combines all these dimensions in perfect proportions and balance, with no single dimension overpowering another, and no single right being compromised to fulfill other rights.

Biography of Muḥammad Wāḍiḥ Rashīd Nadwī

They asked: Who taught you Islamic thought? I replied: Our teacher Sayyid Muḥammad Wāḍiḥ Rashīd Nadwī. They said: Give us his biography. I replied: You are asking me to give you a biography of a teacher beloved to me and influential upon me. I've had a long association with him and become very close. By reminding me of him, you have ignited great emotion within me, awakened dormant sadness, and rekindled his love and respect within my soul. I find my pen and mind competing to answer your request, and I do not know which of them will win.

So I begin with a restless pen and active mind: He was the pious scholar, pure and untainted thinker, witty man of letters, shrewd linguist, intelligent and bright thinker, the noble teacher Abū Ja'far Muḥammad Wāḍiḥ Rashīd Nadwī b. Rashīd Aḥmad b. Khalīl al-Dīn Aḥmad b. Rashīd al-Dīn b. Sa'īd al-Dīn Ṣābir b. Ghulām Jīlānī b. Muḥammad Wāḍiḥ b. Muḥammad Ṣābir b. Āyat Allāh b. 'Alam Allāh al-Ḥasanī al-'Alawī al-Nadwī. He was the brother of our teacher the eminent scholar Muḥammad Rābi' Nadwī and the maternal nephew of our shaykh Abū al-Ḥasan 'Alī Nadwī.

He was born 1344/1925 in the village of the Godly scholar Mawlānā 'Alam Allāh Barelvī, in the outskirts of Raebareli. He graduated from Nadwat al-'Ulamā' with an 'ālimiyyah degree and faḍīlah specialization in Arabic literature in 1370/1951. He earned a license in the English language from Aligarh Islamic College and received ijāzah from Shaykh Abū al-Ḥasan 'Alī Nadwī, Mawlānā Muḥammad Zakariyyā Kāndihlawī and Shaykh 'Abd al-Fattāḥ Abū Ghuddah.

He worked for some time for Radio India in Delhi. He became a teacher at the Nadwah in 1393/1973, and during his tenure served as the editor of the newspaper al-Rā'id,[86] co-editor of the periodical al-Ba'th al-Islāmī,[87] rector of the College of Arabic, and rector of the Higher Institute for Da'wah and Islamic Thought. He was entrusted with leadership of the educational department at the Nadwah in 1426/2005.

---

[86] Fortnightly newspaper published in Arabic at Nadwah.
[87] Monthly Arabic magazine issued by Nadwah.

He authored *Qaḍāyā al-fikr al-islāmī, Adab al-ṣaḥwah al-islāmiyyah, al-Shi'r al-islāmī, Manhaj 'ulamā' al-hind fī tarbiyah al-Islāmiyyah,* and many other beneficial books, along with hundreds of articles on various topics in Arabic and Urdu.

He excelled in knowledge and practice, and combined intelligence with wisdom and good character. He was a model of humility, sublime manners, abstention from vain pastimes, safeguarding time, brevity of speech and social interaction, and aloofness from ostentation and ceremony. He was devoted to teaching and training students, pouring out his love for them, advising them and remaining open and free for them. People were unanimous in acknowledging his virtues, merits and praises, because eyes had simply not seen his equivalent.

I read to him parts of his brother's book *al-Adab al-'arabī bayna 'arḍ wa naqd* and *al-Fikr al-islāmiyyah* of Muḥammad Mubārak. I also learned from him many lessons in Arabic literature, composition, writing, and intellectual struggle. I also benefited greatly from numerous sittings with him in his office at al-Rā'id. I was keen on spending my spare time in his office, where we used to peruse the pages of newspapers and Arabic volumes and hear his analysis of Islamic issues and his interpretation of current Arab affairs.

I heard from him the 'First Ḥadīth' (al-ḥadīth al-musalsal bi al-awwaliyyah)[88] in my home in Oxford on the 4th of Jamādī al-Ākhirah 1421/2000, and he granted me ijāzah in it. During the course of my i'tikāf in the mosque of Takiyyat Kulān in Raebareli in Ramadan 1433/2012, I heard from him the musalsal ḥadīth narrations of al-awwaliyyah, al-muṣāfaḥah and al-aswadayn.[89] In his ijāzah to me, he wrote the following:

> With the name of God, Most Gracious, Most Merciful. Peace and blessings upon the leader of the Messengers and seal of the Prophets Muḥammad and upon all his family and companions. As to what follows: The honorable brother Dr. Moḥammad Akram Nadwī, may God preserve him, requested from me ijāzah in ḥadīth, particularly the musalsal narrations. I am not deserving of that at all, but I do have the honor of attending some lessons of the great ḥadīth scholar and Godly reformer Mawlānā Muḥammad Zakariyyā Kāndihlawī of Madīnah, God's mercy be upon him, and participation in his narration of the musalsal narrations. I

[88] See previous chapter.
[89] Ibid.

was also the student of Mawlānā Ḥalīm 'Aṭā' the shaykh of ḥadīth in Nadwat al-'Ulamā'. It pleases me to grant him ijāzah in order to connect him to this golden thread, and that gives me great pleasure. I ask God to make me worthy of this and to give Dr. Akram Nadwī, through the grace of his service to Prophet ḥadīth, even more success in serving this discipline as well as Islām and Muslims in general. I ask God to bless his efforts, and God is the granter of all success.

They asked: What were your teacher's distinctions in Islamic thinking? I replied: I have not seen anyone that approached his level in explaining the historical progression of Islamic thought and the need to purify it from external and foreign influences. I saw him as excelling specifically in the following points:

1. Accurate academic presentation of the historical struggle between pure Islamic thought and contrived Western thought in all its philosophical and intellectual manifestations taken from its materialistic outlook on life and existence.
2. Truthful and realistic study of the Western cultural war targeting the elements and foundations of Islamic culture, as well as its origins and branches.
3. Balanced and academic analysis of imported solutions and their intellectual, cultural and civilizational effects on the Islamic world.
4. Fairness and moderation in weighing the views of Muslim thinkers without any prejudice, bias, or fanaticism.

They asked: Tell us more about the merits and virtues of your teacher, for we always find you referring to him and becoming pleased in remembering him. I replied: He was an esteemed teacher and source of pride for Nadwat al-'Ulamā'. He arrived at correct views spontaneously. He was extremely serious and joked very little. He was frequently silent, as if silence were a deliberate part of his conduct and manners. His lessons in class were highly organized and arranged in clear sections and hierarchies. He would link all subsidiary matters with their universals, and his methodology was very clear. His words in various settings were like scattered jewels and pearls, but at the same time, they were eloquently composed and comprehensive in meaning, and well-received and understood by others. We would plant them within ourselves, and they would penetrate our depths. I recall so many of them on various occasions.

The most valuable thing he possessed was his profound and serious thinking, the most noble thing his excellent and elevated character, and the sweetest things was his subdued and gentle voice which was like music to our ears striking into the depths of our hearts and minds. His assemblies would bring new intellectual and literary insights to us every day. He was not one to repeat himself. He used to continually read and study in order to increase his knowledge, which he would then pour down upon us. He had an abiding influence upon me, and many of his words were etched into my mind, memorized in youth but continuing to benefit me as the years progress. Every time I remember his assemblies or classes, I find my soul yearning for them and regretting their passing. Until recently, I used to advise the students at Nadwat al-'Ulamā' to take advantage of his presence, learning from him, seeking ijāzah from him, and benefitting from his humility, composure and refined conduct.[90] Few are scholars who are knowledgeable and sincere, while being adorned with lofty character.

They asked: Why are you so profuse in this praise of his? I replied: Pardon me, but my heart is filled with love for him. I have wonderful and fond memories of him which I cherish and which push me to keep on remembering him. Whatever I received from him I consider far too little. I have found people's praise for him to be far greater than the praise of the greatest kings, and his acclaim greater than that of conquering warriors. Whenever I remember him profusely, I find it lacking and insufficient. I covet his disdain for the world and everything it contains, and his independence from all that people pounce upon and are envious of.

---

[90] These words were penned while the shaykh was still alive.

13

WHO TAUGHT YOU HOW TO THINK CRITICALLY

They asked: What is critical thinking? I replied: The faculty of critical thinking is basically the process of analogical deduction, which consists of drawing order and connection between things and matters, linking the known with the unknown, and that which is understood with that which is less understood. Sound critical thinking emanates from correct ordering and precise linking between various issues, such as causes with their effects; results with their reasons or rationale; starting premises with their end results; and fundamental principles with their subsidiary, peripheral issues. This must be done in such a manner that the path and link through these components and parts becomes explicitly clear and firmly established.

If that process lacks any clarity or precision, this will indicate a lack of discovering the true linkages between parts and elements. Moreover, it can also be proof of deficient and foolish composition, or even a corrupt and imagined arrangement of concepts and issues. This type of thinking can often resemble the associations found in one's dreams—specious and chaotic as they often are—which rarely lead to a complete and harmonious meaning upon waking. Sound and harmonious meaning can only arise by resorting to persistent and exhaustive efforts in thinking and observation.

They asked: Is all critical thinking the same type? I replied: No. There are two basic types of critical thinking: the first being the general thinking and observations of those who are intelligent and wise; and second, the observations of the specialists of various advanced disciplines and arts, such as philosophers, theologians and jurists.

They asked: What is the difference between them? I replied: Both are essential and important. We need the first type of thinking in all of life's endeavors and what generally affects us in most states and circumstances. We must rely on the second type when we study specific advanced disciplines, so that we don't wind up muddling scattered and opposite ideas, or separating equivalent and similar concepts.

Biography of Shahbāz Iṣlāḥī

They asked: From whom did you learn this type of thinking? I replied: I have learned it from many teachers of mine, but perhaps I am most indebted to our teacher Mawlānā Shahbāz Iṣlāḥī, may God have mercy on him. I have not met a thinker of his likes, in the East or in the West, from Muslim thinkers or others.

They asked: We never find you tiring of mentioning his grace upon you. We wish you would present to us a glimpse from his life. I replied: He is the eminent scholar, noble Qur'ānic commentator, and unique thinker Shahbāz Iṣlāḥī b. Muḥammad Ḥabīb b. Alṭāf Ḥusayn b. Ni'mat Miān. He was a brilliant and insightful scholar who possessed penetrating and profound insights. Some of his ancestors worked as judges in Jawnpūr during the days of the righteous Mughal ruler Aurangzeb. His father Muḥammad Ḥabīb was from the wealthy people of his time, loved by Muslim as well as Hindū residents of his village. He himself loved those who were pious, and was a follower of Mawlānā Āsī Ghāzīpūrī.[91] He had established a school to meet the educational and religious needs of Muslims.

Mawlānā Shahbāz was born in India in the village of Bijehata in the district of Sīwān in the state of Biḥār, in approximately the year 1348/1930. He began his studies under his brother and local scholars of his village. His brother participated in the Indian freedom movement, being involved at a secondary level.

He studied the works of the author Abū al-A'lā Mawdūdī (d. 1399/1979) and was greatly influenced and impressed by him. He left his secular studies at the official schools for the religious school at Kānpūr, and, after a year, enrolled in the Iṣlāḥī seminary in Serā'ī Mīr in Azamgarh, on the 5th of Dhū al-Qi'dah in 1366/1947. He graduated from there on the 24th of Sha'bān 1370/1951. He had studied under Ṣadr al-Dīn Iṣlāḥī, Jalīl Aḥsan Nadwī, Muṣṭafā Nadwī, 'Ubaydullah Raḥmānī and others. He also spent time under the particular tutelage of Akhtar Aḥsan Iṣlāḥī, student of the renowned scholar Imām Ḥamīd al-Dīn Farāhī, gaining from him the thought and methodology of Farāhī in tafsīr. He also narrated from the reciter Muḥammad Ṭayyib Qāsimī, Shaykh Abū al-Ḥasan 'Alī Nadwī and Shaykh 'Abd al-Fattāḥ Abū Ghuddah, all of whom had granted him a general Ijāzah.

---

[91] A revered and pious Muslim scholar and poet, who died in Ghāzīpūrī in 1335/1917.

He became renowned and preeminent in languages, which included not only Arabic, Persian and Urdu, but also English. He was known for his mastery in Qur'ānic exegesis, Qur'ānic sciences, ḥadīth, fiqh, mathematics, economics, politics, poetry, prosody and literary criticism. He had committed to memory hundreds of verses of Urdu and Persian poetry and was a renowned poet of Urdu himself.

He was preoccupied with da'wah and reform, through writing and teaching. In the end, he had stopped all of these activities except for teaching. He never tired from helping and benefiting students. He taught at the Falāḥ Seminary in Azamgarh, later at the Islamic seminary in Bhatkal, and finally at Nadwat al-'Ulamā', where he began teaching in 1397/1977. He never took a vacation or break except for the days he became ill.

He had pledged[92] to the devout scholar Waṣiyyullāh Fataḥpūrī and later to Abū al-Ḥasan 'Alī Nadwī. He also became a companion of Mawlānā Sa'īd Aḥmad Khān of Azamgarh, the devout scholar Abrār al-Ḥaqq, and the devout scholar Muḥammad Ṣiddīq Bāndwī.

Mawlānā Shahbāz was otherworldly and greatly humble, a lover of knowledge and its seekers. He was sincere and far from seeking fame for his own self or desiring any position of leadership. He preferred instead an austere life, opting to serve students and others.

I read to him *Uṣūl al-Shāshī*,[93] the tafsīr of Sūrah al-Fātiḥah, the Book of Fasting and I'tikāf from the Muwaṭṭa' of Imām Mālik, the Book of Zakāh and the *Muqaddimah* from Ṣaḥīḥ Muslim, and the Book of Etiquette from the Sunan of Abū Dāwūd. I attended his circles and accompanied him for a long period of time. I discussed with him many academic, literary, intellectual and political matters, and wound up adopting many of his views. I was honored by the many letters he wrote to me personally, in which he answered many of my questions. He inspired me to learn and research. In my personal study and training, I owe a massive debt to him which I can never forget. May God give him the best reward.

He granted me Ijāzah in all of his transmissions on the 24th of Rabī' al-Awwal in the year 1419/1998, in a letter he sent to me. I don't think that he ever granted anyone else Ijāzah. He passed on to the mercy of God on the 3rd of Ramaḍān in the year 1423/2002, leaving behind no one like him.

---

92 In the field of taṣawwuf, this refers to the religious pledge known as *bay'ah* which is expressed by students and followers at the hands of their spiritual guides.

93 A primer in Ḥanafī fiqh authored by Imām Niẓām al-Dīn al-Shāshī.

They asked: What was the extent of his observation and thinking? I replied: He reached the heights of intellectual thinking. He never followed another person in any science or thought but researched every matter for himself, especially in tafsīr. Perhaps India itself has not seen one of his likes in understanding the Book of God the Exalted after Imām Ḥamīd al-Dīn Farāhī.

They asked: What is his methodology in thinking? I replied: It was thorough investigation, full examination of suppositions, probing, and proper division and ordering. He used to gather various parts and elements together, isolate their characteristics, and then analyze them academically and precisely, presenting every description, rationale or dimension in its true balance. He would utilize only the most appropriate descriptions, the most harmonious rationales and the most suitable dimensions. He was the farthest from muddled thinking, able to bring together congruous and homogeneous elements and separate incongruous and contradictory elements.

They asked: What was his way of teaching you correct thinking? I replied: He followed two ways, both of them benefiting us in ways whose full extents cannot be described.

They asked: What were they? I replied: The first was by revealing some of the faults in the positions held by previous scholars, philosophers and wise men. He would pose a question to us about the meaning of a verse, ḥadīth, subsidiary fiqh matter, opinion, thought, issue or case; and then commission us to come up with proof for one particular view over another. He would then proceed to expose for us the flaws and defects in our argument. We would then substitute those with other views which we would defend, and he in turn would deconstruct and nullify those. Whatever view or statement we presented, whether it was borrowed from previous scholars or arrived at independently, he would scrutinize in an academic and persuasive way.

The second way was by presenting what he considered to be the right position and proving it through texts and rational evidences, relying on only the most lucid proofs and most vivid evidences.

Whenever we encountered a question, problem or objection to any of his views, he would explain them clearly, starting from their very foundations and establish them clearly and systematically, thereby removing our misgivings completely.

They asked: Could he be characterized by any of the flaws that so commonly affect those who debate and argue? I replied: Absolutely not, for his arguments were academic and tranquil, delivered in a manner that was always courteous, mature, patient and tolerant. He never obliged us to follow any single view of his. He was free from fanaticism towards any juristic, theological or intellectual school, and far above the need to quarrel, argue or be obstinate.

I concluded: Reflect over what I have described to you from the Shaykh's manner, train yourself in academic thinking and devote yourself to it completely.

14

WHO TAUGHT YOU QUR'ĀNIC EXEGESIS

Meanings of the Terms Tafsīr and Ta'wīl

They asked: What is the meaning of exegesis (tafsīr) and interpretation (ta'wīl)? I replied: Tafsīr means to elaborate and uncover, and in the context of the Qur'ān, it means to elaborate on and uncover the meanings of the verses and texts of the Qur'ān. Ta'wīl, on the other hand, is to refer a statement back to its actual meaning, and in the context of the Qur'ān, ta'wīl would be to elaborate on the external realities to which the verses and texts of the Qur'ān refer. But it should be understood that these terms have been used in varying ways by scholars. Ibn Taymiyyah, for instance, states:

> The word ta'wīl has been used lexically for three meanings:
>
> Firstly, the usage of many later scholars of scholastic theology (kalām) who were concerned with jurisprudence and its foundational principles is that ta'wīl refers to diverting a word from its obvious meaning to a less obvious meaning based upon some evidence or indicators. This is the usage of most of those who discussed the term in the context of God's attributes—for instance, whether ta'wīl was to be done with God's attributes or abandoned, or whether it was praiseworthy or blameworthy in this context, or whether it was absolutely correct or false.
>
> Secondly, the usage of most commentators of the Qur'ān is that ta'wīl is simply synonymous with tafsīr. Ibn Jarīr and other commentators often use the expression: "The scholars of ta'wīl have differed on this." Mujāhid is the leader of the scholars of tafsīr, and Imām al-Thawrī said, "If you obtain the tafsīr of Mujāhid, it would be sufficient for you." His tafsīr is relied upon by Shāfi'ī, Aḥmad b. Ḥanbal, Bukhārī and others. When it is mentioned, for instance, that he knows the ta'wīl of

> the unclear verses, what is meant is that he knows their tafsīr (interpretation).
>
> The third usage of ta'wīl is for the ultimate reality that the words refer to. As God says, *"Are they but waiting for the final meaning (ta'wīl) of that [Day of Judgment] to unfold? [But] on the Day when its final meaning is unfolded, those that have neglected it before will say: 'The Messengers of Our Lord did indeed bring forth the truth.'"*[94] So the ta'wīl of what is in the Qur'ān concerning the news of the Resurrection means that which God informs us about—from the Day of Judgment, the Accounting, the Reward, Paradise, Hellfire and their likes. It is as He says in the story of Yūsuf where his parents and brothers prostrated before him: *"O my father! This is the real meaning (ta'wīl) of my dream of long ago !"*[95] Here, God deemed the ta'wīl of the dream to be precisely what was found externally (i.e. its external reference or reality).[96]

They asked: What is the need for tafsīr? I replied: It is well known that God addresses His creation in a manner than can be understood. For this reason, He sent every prophet and revelation in the language of its people. The Qur'ān was revealed in plain Arabic to an era where people had perfected the eloquence of language. They understood very well all the overt rules and manifestations of the language, but its inner details mostly became apparent to them after research, deliberation, and asking the Prophet, peace be upon him. Some of these questions find mention in the Qur'ān itself, but most of them are contained in the books of ḥadīth and Qur'ānic exegesis. Today, we have the same basic needs as the first addressees of the Qur'ān, along with additional requirements due to our shortcomings in language.

Most Important Tafsīr Works

They asked: What are the best books of Qur'ānic exegesis? I replied: Many types of books have been authored in Qur'ānic exegesis. Some of them

---

[94] Qur'ān 7:53.

[95] Qur'ān 12:100.

[96] Pg. 37. Volume 3. Ibn Taymiyyah. *Majmū' al-fatāwā*. Manṣūrah, Egypt: Dār al-Wafā'. 3rd edition. 1426/2005.

involve predominantly transmission of reports from the Prophet, Companions, Followers and other predecessors. These include the exegetical works of Ibn Mājah, Ibn Abī Ḥātim, Ibn Mardawayh, Ibn al-Mundhir, Ibn Jarīr (Ṭabarī), and Baghawī. Others focused on derived views and extensive reasoning. These include the works of the Mu'tazilah,[97] philosophers and other deviant groups. Yet other works focused on uncovering hidden, inner meanings, such as the works of the scholars of taṣawwuf. Exegetical works that focused on jurisprudence included the *Aḥkām al-Qur'ān* works of Shāfi'ī, Jaṣṣāṣ al-Rāzī, Abū Bakr Ibn al-'Arabī, and Qurṭubī. Finally, there were the exegetical works of grammarians and linguists, such as Zajjāj, Wāḥidī, and Abū Ḥayyān. But I will list the most important works of the two main genres of transmission-oriented and reason-oriented works:

The most important transmission-oriented works are:

1. Tafsīr of Ibn Jarīr al-Ṭabarī: This is the work of the imām, luminary, and jurist Abū Ja'far Muḥammad b. Jarīr b. Yazīd al-Ṭabarī, who died 310/923 in Baghdad. He said, "For three years prior to working on it, I petitioned and supplicated God for help in compiling a work of exegesis, and God did help me."
2. Tafsīr of Ibn 'Aṭiyyah: He is the imām, eminent scholar, and master of the Qur'ānic commentators, Abū Muḥammad 'Abd al-Ḥaqq b. Abū Bakr Ghālib b. 'Aṭiyyah al-Muḥāribī of Granada (d. 541/1146).
3. Tafsīr of Ibn Kathīr: He was the great noble scholar and ḥadīth expert 'Imād al-Dīn Abū al-Fidā' Ismā'īl b. 'Umar b. Kathīr, of Qurayshī lineage, from Buṣrah and Damascus (d. 774/1373). His work is one of the best transmission-based works, for he explains the Qur'ān with other verses and with the soundest transmissions from the Prophet and Companions, and from those that followed after them (though it is not void of some weak narrations). His book continues to be a reference for scholars and students of knowledge due to its comprehensive scope, accuracy, precision and soundness.

The most important reason-based works are:

[97] An early theological school that prioritized reason over revelation and often disparaged ḥadīth reports.

1. Al-Tafsīr al-Kashshāf: He was the leader in Arabic language, grammar and expression, and great Mu'tazilite scholar Abū al-Qāsim Maḥmūd b. 'Umar b. Muḥammad al-Zamakhsharī of Khawārizm (d. 538/1144). His work is distinguished by containing great insights in rhetorical eloquence, Arabic language, meaning and expression. In fact, in this domain, the rest of the world is entirely dependent upon his work. Had his work not been marred by his Mu'tazilite views and the distortion of many verses to fit them, it would have been one of the best exegetical works. But despite that, scholars still cannot avoid this work. Ibn Taymiyyah says: "As for Zamakhsharī, then his exegetical work is filled with innovations and the Mu'tazilite way of denying God's attributes, denial of the vision of God in the Hereafter, belief in the createdness of the Qur'ān, denial that God has a will in creation or that He created the actions of His servants, and other Mu'tazilite doctrines."[98]
2. Al-Tafsīr al-Ka'bīr: He is the master of philosophers and scholastic theology Fakhr al-Dīn Muḥammad b. 'Umar b. al-Ḥusayn al-Rāzī of Qurayshī lineage, who died in Herāt in 606/1209. Suyūṭī says in al-Itqān about Rāzī's exegetical work: "His exegetical work is filled with sayings of wise men and philosophers, leading from one thing to another, until the reader finds himself astonished at how far removed the results often are from the original verses." Abū Ḥayyān in al-Baḥr says: "Rāzī has gathered in his work many lengthy things that were unnecessary in the domain of Qur'ānic exegesis." Some scholars have even said, "It contains everything except tafsīr!"

They asked: Who taught you Qur'ānic exegesis? I replied: Our teacher Shahbāz Iṣlāḥī, Burhān al-Dīn Sunbhulī, and Muḥammad 'Ārif Sunbhulī Nadwī. They said: Tell us about their biographies. I replied: I have already

[98] Pg. 386. Volume 13. Ibn Taymiyyah. *Majmū' al-fatāwā*. Madīnah, Saudi Arabia: Majma' al-Mālik Fahd. 1425/2004.

described Shahbāz Iṣlāḥī in a previous chapter, but I will tell you about the others:

Biography of Burhān al-Dīn Sambhalī

He was the great Qur'ānic commentator and jurist Muḥammad Burhān al-Dīn Sambhalī son of the Qur'ānic reciter and physician Ḥamīd al-Dīn Qāsimī. He was born in Dhū al-Ḥijjah 1356/1938 in the city of Sambhal in India. From his father, he attained instruction in Urdu and Persian languages, and the memorization and reading of the Qur'ān. His education took him to various local schools, until he joined Dār al-'Ulūm of Deoband and graduated from there in 1377/1957.

He heard the first portions of Ṣaḥīḥ Bukhārī from Shaykh al-Islām Ḥusayn Aḥmad Madanī and completed the Ṣaḥīḥ with Mawlānā Fakhr al-Dīn. He completed Ṣaḥīḥ Muslim and Sunan Tirmidhī with Mawlānā Ibrāhīm of Balya,[99] and Shāh Walīullah's *Ḥujjatullāh al-bālighah*, the ḥadīth musalsal al-aswadayn[100] and portions of *Mishkāt al-maṣābīḥ* with Mawlānā Muḥammad Ṭayyib al-Qāsimī. He read Sunan Abū Dāwūd with Mawlānā Fakhr al-Dīn, Sunan al-Nasā'ī with Mawlānā Bashīr Aḥmad Khān, *Mishkāt al-maṣābīḥ* with Mawlānā Jalīl Aḥmad of Kayrāna,[101] Muwaṭṭa' through the transmission of Muḥammad b. al-Ḥasan al-Shaybānī (and likely the transmission of Yaḥyā b.Yaḥyā) with Mawlānā Ẓahūr Aḥmad 'Uthmānī, Ṭaḥāwī's *Sharḥ ma'ānī al-āthār* upon Mawlānā Sayyid Ḥasan, Shamā'il Tirmidhī upon Mawlānā 'Abd al-Aḥad, *Hidāyat al-fiqh* with Mawlānā Ḥabīb Aḥmad Isra'īlī Sambhalī, and the last two portions of *al-Hidāyah* with Mawlānā Mi'rāj al-Ḥaqq.

He received ijāzah from the eminent scholar and ḥadīth expert Muḥammad Zakariyyā Kāndihlawī after reading to him *al-Faṣl al-mubīn*, *al-Durar al-thamīn*, and *al-Nawādir min aḥādīth sayyid al-awā'il wa al-awākhir*. He also received ijāzah from Mawlānā Muḥammad Ṭayyib Qāsimī, Ẓahūr Aḥmad 'Uthmānī, 'Abd al-Fattāḥ Abū Ghuddah, Sayyid Fakhr al-Ḥasan, Bashīr Aḥmad, Muḥammad Jalīl Kayrānwī, al-Sayyid Ḥasan Deobandī, and 'Abd al-Aḥad Deobandī.

---

[99] City in the Indian state of Madhya Pradesh.
[100] See previous chapter.
[101] Historic city in the Indian state of Uttar Pradesh.

He taught at the School of Higher Arabic in Fataḥpūr near Delhi for ten months and was then assigned to the education department at Nadwat al-'Ulamā' in 1390/1970.

I learned from him the tafsīr of the Qur'ān from sūrah al-Fātiḥah to al-Mā'idah, portions of Ṣaḥīḥ Muslim, and Shāh Walīullah's *Ḥujjatullāh al-bālighah*. He granted me a general ijāzah in tafsīr, ḥadīth, fiqh on the 25th of Jamādī al-Ūlā in 1422/2001.

Biography of Muḥammad 'Ārif Sambhalī

Our other teacher is the scholar, Qur'ānic commentator, and theologian Mawlānā Muḥammad 'Ārif Sambhalī, who happened to be the nephew of the renowned scholar Muḥammad Manẓūr Nu'mānī. He graduated from Nadwat al-'Ulamā' and taught at schools in Maharashtra and al-Rashād School in Azamgarh. He was ultimately invited by Shaykh Abū al-Ḥasan to Nadwah and delegated to teach Qur'ānic exegesis and theology.

He was distinguished from his peers by his love for the Qur'ān and his unique methodology of Qur'ānic exegesis which was centered upon the concept of tawḥīd and the names and attributes of God. He would elaborate in detail on God's transcendence and purity from every innovated or bad understanding. He would expose the realities and dangers of shirk with all of its subtypes. He would avoid excessively delving into linguistic, grammatical, rhetorical, and juridical aspects of the Qur'ān. He would avoid Judaica[102] and speculative theological matters. His only concern was anchoring the love of God's Book and the ability to experience its meanings and lessons into the hearts of students. He loved to share the issues and understandings that God had opened up for him from the meanings and sciences of the Qur'ān.

He was known for his continual preaching, debating and persistence on the single issue of tawḥīd along with fighting innovations and evil practices. He authored a book, published in several editions, refuting those who frequented shrines out of love for their saints and pious leaders, and those who inappropriately elevated or sanctified them. The most beloved and influential book for him was *Taqwiyat al-īmān* of the martyr Shāh Ismā'īl.

[102] *Isrā'īliyyāt* (translated as Judaica, Judeo-Christian lore, or Israelite narrations) is the term for all reports and material from Judeo-Christian sources that was quoted in Muslim works, especially those on Qur'ānic exegesis.

He was adorned with the loftiest aspirations and the noblest character traits, such as love for the pious, austerity in living, simplicity of food, drink and clothing, abstinence, purity, humility, shunning desires, and being far from affectation.

He died on 13th of Jamādī al-Ūlā 1427/2006.

15

WHO TAUGHT YOU ḤADĪTH

My Personal Journey in Ḥadīth Studies

They asked: Tell us about the beginning of your journey in the noble Prophetic ḥadīth. I replied: When I attained the ʿālimiyyah degree from Dār al-ʿUlūm Nadwat al-ʿUlamāʾ in 1401/1981, I then enrolled in the faḍīlah program, which is basically a specialization in tafsīr, ḥadīth, fiqh, and Arabic literature. At first, I used to view the science of jurisprudence as the most appropriate for scholars due to the great need of people for jurists to teach them the matters of their religion, or their need for muftīs to solve their problems and cases. But after consulting my teachers and guides, it was fated for me to choose ḥadīth as the subject of my specialization. It was a turning point in my life and a new trajectory in my way of thinking and outlook. I studied the entirety of Ṣaḥīḥ Bukhārī with full comprehension, along with Ibn Ṣalāḥ's *Muqaddimah* in detail, as well as other sources and references in this discipline. The love for Ṣaḥīḥ Bukhārī deeply settled in my heart. The subject of my dissertation was the tafsīr of Bukhārī which I compiled from his Ṣaḥīḥ. I also learned in this stage the *Muqaddimah* of Ṣaḥīḥ Muslim and portions of it from our teacher, the proficient researcher Shahbāz Iṣlāḥī. He made it clear to us that Muslim had not criticized Imām Bukhārī nor his teacher ʿAlī b. al-Madīnī in his *Muqaddimah*, as commonly assumed, and that the approach upon which Imām Muslim had claimed historical consensus was in fact the correct one. The stipulation of positive proof for meeting and audition for narrators was an innovated one that was claimed by those who denied ḥadīth, and that this view had become extinct.[103] This view of our shaykh was

[103] This is in reference to a fine point in narrator evaluation: Imām Muslim was responding to a circulating claim that there must exist historical evidence of a narrator meeting his teacher from whom he narrates (and that their being contemporary to one another was insufficient) in order to accept that particular isnād. It was supposed that this stricter criteria belonged to Bukhārī, and that Muslim was harshly criticizing his own teacher. The truth is that both Bukhārī and Muslim had the same criteria, and this artificial addition stipulation was unreasonable and put forward by those who sought to eliminate most, if not all, ḥadīth.

unique, and unprecedented among the teachers of Islamic schools and seminaries. When I mentioned this view to our shaykh 'Abd al-Fattāḥ Abū Ghuddah at a much later time, he found it odd that some teachers in India had reached the same conclusion that he had also reached.

When I graduated from Nadwah I immediately became a teacher there. During the course of my teaching, we were sent to King Saud University in Riyad in 1406/1985-6 for an educational program of four-month duration. I took this opportunity to benefit from our shaykh 'Abd al-Fattāḥ—prior to that I had attended his lectures as a visiting scholar to Nadwah. He not only recognized me but warmly welcomed me into his home in Riyad. Thereafter, I would frequently visit his home like a person thirsty for water. I read to him many things and benefited from his upright conduct, behavior and character. He wrote his ijāzah for me in his own handwriting on three separate occasions. I was so pleased with his ijāzah that, for a time, I did not seek ijāzah from anyone else at all, except what I already possessed from our shaykh Abū al-Ḥasan.

Then Shaykh Abū al-Ḥasan sent me as a researcher to Oxford University in 1411/1990. In its library, Dhahabī's book *Siyar a'lām al-nubalā'* caught my attention. I borrowed it and read the entire work, becoming totally engrossed in it. I loved it so much that I eventually purchased a copy for myself and read it again. In the end, I had read it several times. I began to love ḥadīth and its scholars, and the idea of isnād and ijāzah. I also studied in the library the ḥadīth expert 'Abd al-Ḥayy al-Kittānī's *Fahras al-fahāris*—and I had not heard of this author or this book before. After reading this work multiple times, I was inspired to seek ijāzah and those scholars possessing isnāds. I was honored to meet a number of young people of ḥadīth in the Arab world with whom I developed close bonds. This is how ḥadīth and isnād became my passion and hobby, and praise is for God.

They asked: Who taught you ḥadīth at Nadwat al-'Ulamā'? I replied: Our teachers Mawlānā Shahbāz Iṣlāḥī, Mawlānā 'Abd al-Sattār A'ẓamī, Mawlānā Ḍiyā' al-Ḥasan Nadwī, and Mawlānā Muḥammad Zakariyyā Sunbhulī.

They said: Give us their biographies. I replied: I have already described one, but I will tell you about the rest.

Biography of ʿAbd al-Sattār Aʿẓamī

Mawlānā ʿAbd al-Sattār Aʿẓamī was a great scholar and noble ḥadīth expert who was born and raised in Mau in the outskirts of Azamgarh. He graduated from Maẓāhir al-ʿUlūm in Sahāranpūr. He learned ḥadīth from the eminent scholar ʿAbd al-Laṭīf of Sahāranpūr. Mawlānā Zakariyyā al-Kāndihlawī, Mawlānā Manẓūr Aḥmad of Sahāranpūr and other scholars.

He taught at Nadwat al-ʿUlamāʾ for a number of years, where I read to him the Books of Faith and Knowledge from Ṣaḥīḥ Bukhārī, the Books of Purity and Prayer from Sunan Tirmidhī, and portions from Sunan Ibn Mājah. He used to love me greatly and would lend me his copies of various ḥadīth commentaries, while warning me about Ibn Ḥajar. He used to believe that reading Ibn Ḥajar's *Fatḥ al-Bārī* had a potential negative effect on students and would turn me away from the Ḥanafī school or reduce its standing my eyes.

He authored a commentary on Sunan Tirmidhī which he utilized in order to teach us. He would do this while defending the Ḥanafī school and disparaging the others. He would disagree with most commentators very strongly, including the ḥadīth expert Ibn Ḥajar, the eminent ḥadīth scholar ʿAbd al-Raḥmān Mubārakpūrī, and the great and noble ḥadīth scholar Aḥmad Muḥammad Shākir. He would also refute the Ahl al-Ḥadīth scholars of India[104] like the eminent scholar of ḥadīth Nadhīr Ḥusayn Dihlawī and all who were similar to him. His refutation of them was in a number of peripheral matters and juridical issues. In this arena, you would hear his loud voice and prolonged breath, and see him like a powerful warrior brandishing his weapons. He would spare no opponent nor have mercy on any dissenter. He would deal with every commentator or presenter with the response of the Ḥanafī school, with which he would uncover their flaws and tear their curtains. He was not unique in this approach, for this is the predominant approach of the schools of India. It was, however, quite strange in the environment of Nadwat al-ʿUlamāʾ, where tolerance in peripheral matters and respect for scholars of differing schools and views was the norm.

---

104 The *ahl-e-ḥadīth,* Urdu-language form of the term *ahl al-ḥadīth,* refers to a religious group that emerged in India in opposition to the majority Ḥanafī school of jurisprudence. They criticized strict adherence to the legal schools without a concern for the sources of jurisprudence, i.e. ḥadīth. Ḥanafī—Ahl-e-ḥadīth polemics feature prominently in religious discourses in the Indian subcontinent.

I have not been able to compile a complete biography of his nor find his date of demise. May God have mercy on him and raise his ranks, for he was from the pious and sincere scholars.

Biography of Ḍiyā᾿ al-Ḥasan Nadwī

Mawlānā Ḍiyā᾿ al-Ḥasan Nadwī was an eminent scholar and ḥadīth researcher who was the son of the ḥadīth expert ʿAbd al-Ḥayy al-Mi'awī al-Aʿẓamī. He was born in Ramadan 1350/1932 in Mau, now known as Maunath Bhanjan. He studied at the Miftāḥ al-ʿUlūm school and learned from the ḥadīth scholar Mawlānā Ḥabīb al-Raḥmān Aʿẓamī, Mawlānā ʿAbd al-Laṭīf Nuʿmānī Aʿẓamī and Mawlānā Shams al-Dīn Aʿẓamī. He spent three years at Dār al-ʿUlūm Deoband where he learned Ṣaḥīḥ Bukhārī from Shaykh al-Islām Ḥusayn Aḥmad Madanī and other common books from various teachers. He joined the department of Arabic literature at Nadwat al-ʿUlamā᾿ in the year 1373/1954 and took from our Mawlānā Muḥammad Rābiʿ Ḥasanī Nadwī, Dr. ʿAbdullah ʿAbbās Nadwī, ʿAbd al-Mājid Nadwī, and our teacher Abū al-ʿIrfān Nadwī.

He was called to Beirut by his teacher Mawlānā Ḥabīb al-Raḥmān Aʿẓamī to help him work on the Muṣannaf of ʿAbd al-Razzāq. After that, he traveled to Arabia, Turkey and Malaysia, teaching at various schools until he was appointed at Nadwah in 1395/1975 to teach ḥadīth.

I read to him the entirety of Ṣaḥīḥ Bukhārī, excluding the Book of Faith and Knowledge, with precision and comprehension. He was given the gift of eloquence of expression in his lessons and was always concerned with finding solutions to difficult portions while removing doubts and confusion. He excelled at pinpointing the accurate balance of ḥadīth, fiqh and isnād in his lessons. He did this in great detail, with logical connection and great clarity. I praise him with what the ʿAbbāssid-era poet Abū Ubādah al-Buḥturī (d. 284/897) said:

> Convey meanings like the flower-bud
> which beams in spring's glory, fresh and new.
> Seize aged, borrowed words by choice,
> Evade disorder's daze, all dark and blue.

We would feel the power and force that the noble shaykh expended in bringing forth proofs and evidences, scrutinizing texts through their expressions and implications and returning to sources and commentaries. This was surely an exhausting effort which could not be performed except by those who had been blessed by a massive share of divine felicity and large aptitude for research and investigation. The shaykh had spent a long period of time with ḥadīth, especially Ṣaḥīḥ Bukhārī, which imparted on him a permanent and wonderful aura, and a deep grasp of the aims of Bukhārī. He would promote the study of Ṣaḥīḥ Bukhārī and its chapter divisions, with a sound and sensible order and arrangement. His lessons would not betray any personal whims or prejudices but exhibit only the most profound and deep comprehension of the true meaning of evidences. He would only delve into the battles between scholars with maturity, wide-ranging study and justice. He had given himself up completely for the sake of knowledge and used his knowledge only to make the truth apparent. He had no other preoccupation apart from teaching, reading and benefiting others.

He died on Monday the 15th of Jamādī al-Ūlā in 1409/1988 at the age of fifty-eight, and Nadwat al-'Ulamā' was filled with great sorrow and tremendous pain on that day.

He was a scholar who was deeply versed and skilled in the ḥadīth sciences. He was calm, forbearing and composed. He shunned and rose above anything that would detract from noble characteristics. He was frequently silent, and humble to the point of loving anonymity. He would involve me in some of his research work only in order to train me in that. In his presence, I always sensed a bond and connection that was deeper than that of family. That was the bond of knowledge and ḥadīth. What a pure and pleasant bond that is!

Biography of Muḥammad Zakariyyā Sunbhulī Nadwī

Mawlānā Muḥammad Zakariyyā Sunbhulī Nadwī was a scholar of ḥadīth and jurist who was born on the 21st of Rabī' al-Awwal in 1363/1944. He heard Ṣaḥīḥ Bukhārī from Mawlānā Fakhr al-Dīn, Ṣaḥīḥ Muslim from Mawlānā Bashīr Aḥmad Khān, Sunan Tirmidhī from Mawlānā Ibrāhīm al-Bilyāwī and Mawlānā Fakhr al-Ḥasan, Sunan Abū Dāwūd from Mawlānā Fakhr al-Ḥasan, Sunan Nasā'ī from Mawlānā 'Abd al-Aḥad, Sunan Ibn Mājah from Mawlānā Mi'rāj al-Ḥaqq, Muwaṭṭa' from Mawlānā Sharīf al-Ḥasan, and the Muwaṭṭa' with the transmission of Muḥammad from Mawlānā Ḥāfiẓ al-Nuʿmānī from Bahraich.[105] He also attended the reading of the three texts to Mawlānā Muḥammad Zakariyyā Kāndihlawī and specialized in Arabic literature at Nadwat al-ʿUlamāʾ.

I witnessed the reading of the latter half of Sunan Tirmidhī read upon him, as well as portions of Sunan Nasāʾī and Sunan Ibn Mājah. He granted me a general ijāzah on the 25th of Jamādī al-Ūlā in 1422/2001.

He was one of those teachers at the Nadwah who was beloved in the hearts of students. He confined himself to knowledge and teaching, especially explaining ḥadīth in a manner that was distinguished by its clarity, spontaneity and lack of pretense. He used to give wide-ranging and complete answers for even the most difficult questions and the most ambiguous and insurmountable inquiries. He was the best teacher and advisor, and most virtuous role model.

[105] Town near Lucknow in the state of Uttar Pradesh in India.

16

WHO TAUGHT YOU PRINCIPLES OF ḤADĪTH

They asked: What principles do ḥadīth scholars consider in authenticating or weakening ḥadīth? I replied: I have explained these in a previous monograph which contains it all, as well as a small treatise containing its most important foundations and most basic principles entitled *Mabādi' fī uṣūl al-ḥadīth wa al-isnād ('Foundations in the Principles of Ḥadīth and Isnād').*[106]

They asked: Then what then are the most essential references in the principles and terminology of ḥadīth? I replied: They are the following:

1. *Al-risālah* of Imām Shāfi'ī (d. 204/820)
2. *Muqaddimah* of Muslim (d. 261/875)
3. *Kitāb al-'ilal* of Abū 'Īsā Tirmidhī (d. 279/892)
4. *Al-Muḥaddith al-fāṣil bayna al-rāwī wa al-wā'ī* of Qāḍī Abū Muḥammad al-Ḥasan b. 'Abd al-Raḥmān b. Khallād al-Rāmahurmuzī (d. 360/971)
5. *Ma'rifah 'ulūm al-ḥadīth* of Abū 'Abdullah Muḥammad b. 'Abdullah al-Ḥākim of Nīshāpūr (d. 405/1014)
6. *Al-kifāyah fī 'ilm al-riwāyah* of Abū Bakr Aḥmad b. 'Alī b. Thābit al-Khaṭīb of Baghdad (d. 463/1071)
7. *Muqaddimah 'ulūm al-ḥadīth* of Abū 'Amr 'Uthmān b. 'Abd al-Raḥmān al-Shahrazūrī, better known as Ibn al-Ṣalāḥ (d. 643/1245)
8. *Nukhbat al-fikr fī muṣṭalaḥ ahl al-athar* and its commentary *Nuzhat al-naẓar*, both of them by the ḥadīth expert Ibn Ḥajar of Ashkelon (d. 852/1449)

They asked: What is the best book on transmitters? I replied: the *Tārīkh* of Bukhārī; what has reached us from 'Alī al-Madīnī, Yaḥyā b. Ma'īn, Aḥmad b. Ḥanbal, Ibn Abī Ḥātim al-Rāzī; the works of Ibn Ḥibbān. And all of these are combined in *Tahdhīb al-kamāl* of Abū al-Ḥajjāj al-Mizzī, the proficient ḥadīth expert. In fact, there is nothing in all of Islām that is its equivalent to it.

[106] *Mabādi' fī uṣūl al-ḥadīth wa al-isnād.* London, UK: Al-Salām Institute Press. 1436/2015.

Following these, there are the books of the ḥadīth expert Shams al-Dīn Dhahabī: *Tārīkh al-islām, Siyar aʿlām al-nubalāʾ, Tadhkirat al-ḥuffāẓ, Mīzān al-iʿtidāl* and *al-Mughnī.*

They asked: What is the best work on delineating the sources of ḥadīth? I replied: *Bustān al-muḥaddithīn* of Shāh ʿAbd al-ʿAzīz al-Dihlawī in Persian, which I critically translated into Arabic with some additions. Then there is al-*Risālah al-mustaṭrifah* of one of our senior teachers the eminent scholar and ḥadīth expert Muḥammad b. Jaʿfar al-Kittānī.

Biography of Salmān Ḥusaynī Nadwī

They asked: From whom have you learned the principles of ḥadīth and the study of its transmitters? I replied: I have heard the *Muqaddimah* of Ibn al-Ṣalāḥ and *Bustān al-muḥaddithīn* from our shaykh the ḥadīth scholar Sharīf Salmān Ḥusaynī Nadwī along with detailed explanations.

They said: Give us his biography. I replied: He is the eminent scholar, preacher, ḥadīth scholar, of noble Prophetic lineage, Abū Yūsuf Salmān b. Muḥammad Ṭāhir b. Muḥammad Yūsuf al-Ḥusaynī al-Ḥasanī al-ʿAlawī al-Hāshimī. He was born in 1373/1953 in Lucknow and raised there. After memorizing and perfecting the Qurʾān, he attained the ʿālimiyyah degree in 1394/1974 and the faḍīlah degree in 1396/1976 from Nadwat al-ʿUlamāʾ. He learned Arabic literature from our teachers Muḥammad Rābiʿ Ḥasanī Nadwī, Muḥammad Wāḍiḥ Rashīd Nadwī, and Saʿīd al-Raḥmān Aʿẓamī Nadwī. He read *Hidāyat al-fiqh* of Burhān al-Dīn al-Marghīnānī with our Mawlānā Nāṣir ʿAlī Nadwī, and Shāh Walīullah's *Ḥujjat Allāh al-bālighah* with Mawlānā Burhān al-Dīn Sunbhulī. He also heard Nawawī's *Riyāḍ al-ṣāliḥīn* with Muḥammad Rābiʿ Ḥasanī Nadwī, the first half of *Mishkāt al-maṣābīḥ* with Burhān al-Dīn Sunbhulī who narrated from Fakhr al-Ḥasan, and the second half with Mawlānā Wajīh al-Dīn who narrated from Shāh Ḥalīm ʿAṭāʾ. He heard Ṣaḥīḥ Bukhārī from ʿAbd al-Sattār Aʿẓamī who narrated from ʿAbd al-Laṭīf of Sahāranpūr. He also heard portions of Ṣaḥīḥ Bukhārī from Burhān al-Dīn Sunbhulī and most of Ṣaḥīḥ Muslim. He heard the first half of Sunan Abū Dāwūd from ʿAbd al-Sattār Aʿẓamī, and the second half from Muḥammad Ẓahūr Nadwī. He heard portions of Sunan Nasāʾī, Ibn Mājah and *Maʿānī al-āthār* of Ṭaḥāwī from ʿAbd al-Sattār Aʿẓamī; and the *Muqaddimah* of Ibn al-Ṣalāḥ, and *Bustān al-muḥaddithīn* from Burhān al-Dīn Sunbhulī.

He attended the college of Uṣūl al-Dīn at Imām Muḥammad b. Sa'ūd Islamic University in Riyāḍ and attained his masters in ḥadīth. He also read *Mukhtārāt min al-ṣaḥīḥ* with Shaykh al-Sayyid Muḥammad Nidā of Egypt; and *al-Taṣwīr al-fannī* and *al-Taṣwīr al-mauḍū'ī* with Dr. Ḥasan Farḥāt. He also accompanied Shaykh 'Abd al-Fattāḥ Abū Ghuddah and benefited from him greatly. He read to him Ibn al-Ṣalāḥ's *Muqaddimah* among other things. Shaykh 'Abd al-Fattāḥ was greatly impressed with Mawlānā Salmān and granted him ijāzah on more than one occasion. Mawlānā Salmān was also given ijāzah by his own father in ḥadīth, as general ijāzah was the practice of the people.

Mawlānā Salmān also accompanied the Godly scholar Muḥammad Aḥmad al-Burtābakdhī and benefited from him. He received ijāzah from Shāh Sayyid Nafīs al-Ḥusaynī one of the deputees of Mawlānā 'Abd al-Qādir of Rāipūr in taṣawwuf.

He became a teacher at Nadwat al-'Ulamā' in 1402/1982, where to this day, he continues to teach ḥadīth along with other subjects, and trains students in writing academic research papers. His works include *Ārā' al-imām al-dihlawī fī tārīkh al-tashrī' al-islāmī, Durūs min al-ḥadīth al-nabawī al-sharīf, al-Amānah fī al-Qur'ān, Lamḥah 'an 'Ilm al-jarḥ wa al-ta'dīl, Ḥayāt al-imām al-Bukhārī, al-Ta'rīf al-wajīz bi kutub al-ḥadīth al-sharīf,* and *Khuṭubāt banklor.* He also critically edited *Risālah 'Abd al-Ḥaqq Muḥaddith al-Dihlawī fī al-ḥadīth al-sharīf* and translated Shāh Walīullah's Persian-language work *al-Fawz al-ka'bīr* into Arabic. He also has a wonderful and eloquent translation of the Qur'ān into Urdu, as well as an abridged Qur'ānic commentary in Urdu. He has a commentary on *Mishkāt al-maṣābīḥ* in Arabic, personal memoirs of several volumes in Arabic, and many other works and articles.

I read to him parts of Ibn al-Ṣalāḥ's *Muqaddimah*, and all of *Bustān al-muḥaddithīn*. He dictated to me some matters pertaining to other religions. I also learned from him many matters pertaining to religion and the history of Islamic movements. I accompanied him on many journeys. I continue to be impressed by him and increase in my love for him. I am indebted to him in many aspects of academic training, may God reward him with the best that his pious servants can expect to be rewarded.

He granted me ijāzah in all his transmissions, with the following text:

Praise be to God, Lord of the worlds. Peace and blessings be upon the master of the Messengers Muḥammad, and all his family and companions. As to what follows: My brother in faith has requested ijāzah from me, who is a young and virtuous scholar, a noble and pious researcher, Shaykh Moḥammad Akram Nadwī—may God preserve him, enamor him with skills and abilities, and accept his deeds and his service—in all transmissions from the books of ḥadīth and its branches and sciences. I grant him ijāzah in all that I transmit from my teachers with their isnāds to the authors of these books and to the Messenger of God, peace be upon him. I hope that he increases in his service to the noble Prophetic ḥadīth and its sciences, is successful with what he possesses of knowledge, prepares himself to spread the sciences of the Sharīʿah, and serve the pure Sunnah in word and deed and practice. May God accept from him and from us, and raise us in the company of the pious ones, the protectors of the sunnah and the ones who served this faith, and God is the protector of the pious.

17

WHO TAUGHT YOU JURISPRUDENCE

Meaning of Fiqh

They asked: What is jurisprudence (fiqh)? I replied: It is deep understanding of this religion—in its fundamentals and subsidiary matters, and its universals and particulars—through relying upon God's Book, the sunnah of His Messenger, peace be upon him, and upon the fear of God and self-restraint. Ibn Baṭṭah relates in *Ibṭāl al-Ḥiyal* that Mujāhid said, "The jurist is the one who fears God." Ibn Baṭṭah also relates from Maṭar al-Warrāq: I asked Ḥasan about a matter and he gave the answer. I said to him, "Abū Sa'īd, the jurists deny this." He replied, "May your mother be bereaved of you, O Maṭar. Have you ever seen a jurist at all?" He also said, "Do you know what a real jurist is? The jurist is the one who is cautious, abstinent and steadfast on the way of God's Messenger, peace be upon him. He does not mock those below him or above him, and does not ruin the knowledge that God has taught him."

In the lexicon of later scholars, fiqh is the knowledge of the practical rulings of the Sharī'ah acquired from its detailed evidences. The term fiqh is also used to refer to the totality of these rulings.

History of Fiqh

They asked: When was fiqh developed? I replied: Fiqh developed alongside Islam itself, for Islam is nothing but a combination of faith (īmān), practical rules (aḥkām) and conduct (akhlāq). The Qur'ān was revealed for these three essential components, and the Messenger, peace be upon him, clarified them through his sunnah. After his passing, when the Companions were faced with many new issues that the Qur'ān and Sunnah did not explicitly mention, they endeavored to come up with their own opinions in order to arrive at solutions by referring back to the texts of the Qur'ān and Sunnah in some way. Similarly, the Followers and subsequent generations after them all did the same. The sum totality of all of this represents the discipline of jurisprudence.

They asked: Who was the first to document jurisprudence? I replied: The very first person to refine the issues of jurisprudence, anchor them to their foundational principles, and arrange them into distinct sections was Imām Abū Ḥanīfah al-Nuʿmān b. Thābit of Kūfah (d. 150/767). His jurisprudence was compiled by his companions Abū Yūsuf (d. 182/798) in his various works and Muḥammad b. al-Ḥasan al-Shaybānī (d. 189/805) in his narration-based works such as al-Mabsūṭ, al-Ziyādāt, al-Jāmiʿ al-Ṣaghīr, al-Jāmiʿ al-Kabīr, al-Siyar al-Ṣaghīr, al-Siyar al-Kabīr, and others.

Imām Mālik (d. 179/795) authored the Muwaṭṭa', which represented the the jurisprudence of the people of Madīnah, and then Muḥammad b. Idrīs al-Shāfiʿī (d. 204/820) came and dictated his book al-Umm.

They asked: From whom did you learn jurisprudence? I replied: From Mawlānā Ḥabīb al-Raḥmān Sulṭānpūrī Nadwī and Muftī Muḥammad Ẓahūr Nadwī.

Biography of Ḥabīb al-Raḥmān Nadwī

They said: Give us their biographies. I replied: The first was the shaykh, scholar, accomplished linguist, and great jurist Ḥabīb al-Raḥmān Nadwī son of the scholar Mawlānā ʿAbd al-Raḥmān Sulṭānpūrī, a close associate of Ashraf ʿAlī Thānwī who had left his native Sulṭānpūr to settle in Raebareli where he became a teacher. Our teacher Ḥabīb al-Raḥmān was born in Raebareli in a protected and balanced environment known for seriousness and austerity. This had a great effect on his personality. He was unfamiliar with any pastime or play, and rarely mixed or socialized with people. He learned from his father and other scholars. With the death of his father a new phase began in his life. His passion for knowledge took him to Lucknow where he met the great scholar Mawlānā Muḥammad Asbāṭ, one of the senior teachers at Nadwah. He learned under his tutelage and joined Nadwah, from where he graduated some years later.

He taught at Nadwah for more than fifty years, focusing in particular on teaching books of grammar and Ḥanafī jurisprudence. He would explain matters in exhaustive detail with a loud and generous voice, making plain every letter and word. He was eloquent in expression, and frequent smiles would intersperse his explanations and elaborations. He would answer questions with knowledge-filled and complete answers, but only if they were relevant to the topic. If a student asked a question, however, that was irrelevant to the topic, he would smile and turn away, saying, "A door has now been opened to what's unnecessary and frivolous." Students would enjoy this answer of his.

I read to him the first portion of al-Marghīnānī's *Hidāyat al-Fiqh* with deep comprehension and exhaustive detail. I also served him for a number of months. He was pleased with me and kept me close at hand. He would grant me special time whenever I wanted to understand a difficult issue of jurisprudence, and few students were given that honor.

He got married after the age of fifty—and I don't know the reason for that delay. He was sound-bodied, of abundant strength and energy, and ever youthful. He was by nature inclined to purity, cleanliness and order. He was far removed from any manifestation of modern materialistic culture and civilization. He stayed aloof from people and was cut off from other pursuits, even avoiding conferences and assemblies. However, he was diligent in reading newspapers and journals.

He died in Sultānpūr on the 14th of Rajab 1428/2007 while he was well over eighty years of age. Many of his colleagues and students from Nadwah attended his funeral prayer.

He was greatly humble, abstinent, silent, and avoided socializing. His merits were recognized by others. He was conscious of the value of his time, with extreme precision, not wasting a moment. I observed that whenever Mawlānā Ashraf ʿAlī Thānwī was mentioned, he would weep out of affection. He would become happy when his father's colleagues would visit him. He would honor and love all pious people. He would attend the assemblies of our Shaykh Abū al-Ḥasan after the Aṣr prayer.[107] He used to follow the Sharīʿah and sunnah closely, and was keen on advising students and teaching them exemplary religious conduct. He was one of the most successful and influential teachers. How great is the need for such teachers! How wonderful the words of the master of poets Aḥmad Shawqī concerning teachers:

Surely he's the one to shape the natures right
Surely he's the one to make the souls upright
Surely he's the one that sets the crooked straight
And in every matter, makes them see the stakes
But

[107] The middle prayer among the five mandated prayers, whose time is in the later afternoon.

When the teacher, though, no longer walks
the moral way, through and through
Then its spirit in the young begins to dwindle too
When the teacher, in one eye, is blind of sight
Then from his hands, can hope to come, only of his like.

Biography of Muḥammad Ẓahūr Nadwī

The second is the great scholar, eminent jurist, and muftī Muḥammad Ẓahūr Nadwī A'ẓamī son of 'Abd al-Sattār b. Khān Muḥammad. He was born in 1345/1926 in Mubārakpūr near Azamgarh. He studied elementary books such as the commentary of Mullā Jāmī of Ibn al-Ḥājib's *Kāfiyah*, and the commentary of *al-Tahdhīb fī al-Manṭiq* in the Iḥyā' al-'Ulūm school in Mubārakpūr. He joined Nadwat al-'Ulamā' in 1360/1941, attained the 'ālimiyyah degree in 1366/1947 and the faḍīlah specialization in 1368/1949. He read *Hidāyat al-Fiqh* with his brother-in-law muftī Muḥammad Sa'īd, Mishkāt al-Maṣābīḥ with Mawlānā Isḥāq Sandailwī, Riyāḍ al-Ṣāliḥīn with Mawlānā Muṣṭafā Bustawī, Sharḥ al-Tahdhīb with our teacher the philosopher Abū al-'Irfān Nadwī, Ṣaḥīḥ Bukhārī and Muslim with the ḥadīth scholar Shāh Ḥalīm 'Aṭā', Sunan Abū Dāwūd with Mawlānā Isḥāq Sandailwī, various works of Arabic literature with Mawlānā Muḥammad Nāẓim Nadwī, other works of Arabic literature and Qur'ānic sciences with Shaykh Abū al-Ḥasan 'Alī Nadwī, Sunan Tirmidhī with Mawlānā Sa'īd Aḥmad, Ḥujjat Allāh al-Bālighah with Shāh Ḥalīm 'Aṭā', and Tadarrub (on the rules of issuing rulings) with Muftī Muḥammad Sa'īd (with whom he spent some time).

He began teaching at Nadwah in 1369/1950 and had been working in the department of Iftā' (issuing rulings) since 1375/1955. He was the vice chancellor of the university since 1400/1980 along with being responsible for the Department of Development and Advancement.

I read to him the second half of al-Marghīnānī's Hidāyat al-Fiqh, the Book of Ḥajj from Ṭaḥāwī's Sharḥ Ma'ānī al-Āthār, and al-Sirājī on the rules of inheritance. I was among those that were close to him and spent a large amount of time with him. I visited him at his home in Mubārakpūr and spent one night there with my friend Āftāb 'Ālim Nadwī. He granted me general ijāzah in the sciences of Qur'ān, exegesis, ḥadīth, jurisprudence and fatwā on the 25th of Jamādī al-Ūlā in 1422/2001, and wrote the following:

> Praise be to God, Lord of the worlds. Peace and blessings be upon the master of the Messengers Muḥammad, and all his family and companions. As to what follows: Moḥammad Akram Nadwī read to me portions of Hidāyat al-Fiqh, al-Sirājī, the Book of Ḥajj from Ṭaḥāwī's Sharḥ Ma'ānī al-Āthār, and Tadarrub on issuing rulings. He requested ijāzah, and I have obliged and granted him general ijāzah in the Qur'ānic sciences, exegesis, ḥadīth, fiqh and issuing rulings.

He passed away close to dawn on Sunday, the 13th of Dhū al-Ḥijjah in 1437/2016 at Nadwat al-'Ulamā'. Mawlānā Muḥammad Rābi' Nadwī led his funeral prayer which was attended by unprecedented numbers. There was great sorrow on the news of his demise. He was truly the jurist of his time without dispute. His rulings were characterized by profundity and moderation. He answered questions with evidences and was quick to establish proofs. He was deep-sighted, extremely patient with students and extremely concerned about their affairs. In turn, they reciprocated love for love, and respect for respect.

18

WHO TAUGHT YOU HISTORY

The Importance of Studying History

They asked: Why do you always encourage us to study history? I replied: Knowledge of history is a serious and hefty matter, and one of extreme importance. It involves the review of strategic and developmental factors in human societies, and the study of physical, political, economic and cultural conditions across time and space. No scholar or student of knowledge can afford to be oblivious to it. We learn from history, for example, the context in which Islam was revealed, the monumental changes witnessed by Islamic lands, and the political, cultural and civilizational fluctuations across human traditions. So history is no small or inconsequential discipline, for it concerns our religious and worldly affairs. We simply cannot deny its rightful role in the human sciences, disciplines and crafts.

They said: Some have designated history as being akin to salt in knowledge, which is resorted to only in order to enjoy oneself.[108] What do you say? I replied: They have adopted a repugnant practice and made a dreadful claim. Is there a science whose aim is only to realize mental relaxation, enjoyment or the mere fulfillment of desires? How can that be when all the sciences and disciplines in their totality represent exercising the mind and exertion of power and energy, with little room for laxity or relaxation? Knowledge is attained only through exhausting effort and draining struggle. In this manner, history is one such example of a noble collective human discipline which involves the use of critical thinking and the gathering of matters of great consequence.

They asked: Can you summarize for us the benefit of studying history? I replied: The great philosopher Abū Naṣr al-Fārābī (d. 339/950) summarized it in an amazing way as follows:

---

[108] As salt is used sparingly without being overbearing, in various amounts according to varying tastes, and primarily for enjoyment purposes without representing any significant nutritional value, so too is the discipline of history according to its detractors.

> The most beneficial thing that a person gains from acquiring the knowledge of politics and related disciplines is the ability to reflect and deliberate over the states, actions and dispositions of human beings—either through direct observation or acquired information from others—and the ability to study these carefully in order to distinguish their merits from their faults, and their harmful elements from the beneficial ones. Thereby one endeavors to hold on to that which is good and beneficial in order to attain the same benefits and avoid the harms in order to protect oneself from the same dangers and evils.[109]

They asked: Why don't the Islamic schools in South Asia teach history? I replied: This is the most important and valid criticism of the Niẓāmī curriculum,[110] which has left out or shunned certain important sciences and disciplines whose negligence is condemnable and blameworthy. We have witnessed through experience many graduates of those seminaries who have little knowledge of common and plain matters, or issues related to the life of the Prophet, peace be upon him, his battles, or even Islamic history in general. Our shaykh Abū 'Ammār Zāhid Rāshidī related to us that he has seen some graduates who could not state whether the battle of Badr or Uḥud came first.

Essential References in Islamic History

They said: Tell us about the most essential references in Islamic history. I replied: They are the Noble Qur'ān, books of ḥadīth and battles (maghāzī), books of rankings and genealogy (biographical works), geographical works, personal travelogues and chronicles, books of literature, and Arabic poetry.

---

[109] al-Fārābī, *Risālah fī al-siyāsah al-shar'īyah* ('Treatise on Politics'). See pg. 61, *Al-siyāsah al-shar'īyah: majmū' al-rasā'il*. Beirut, Lebanon: Dār al-Kutub al-'Ilmiyyah. 2003.

[110] The curriculum in religious schools of the Indian subcontinent, referred to as *Dars-e-Niẓāmī*, originated from the sophisticated cosmopolitan culture of Mughal-era Delhi, specifically the Farangī Mahal school established in an abandoned palace left by a European who left no heirs. The palace was gifted by the emperor Aurungzeb to the family of Mullā Quṭb al-Dīn Sihālī, whose son Niẓām al-Din (d. 1161/1748) established the system of education which came to bear his name.

They asked: What are the most important books in general Islamic history? I replied:

1. *Tārīkh al-rusul wa al-mulūk* ('History of Prophets and Kings')[111] of Imām Abū Ja'far Muḥammad b. Jarīr Ṭabarī (d. 310/923)
2. *Murūj al-dhahab wa ma'ādin al-jawhar* ('Meadows of Gold and Mines of Gems'),[112] and *Kitāb al-tanbīh wa al-ashrāf* ('The Book of Admonition and Revision')[113] of Mas'ūdī (d. 346/956)
3. *Tārīkh al-islām* ('The History of Islam') of Dhahabī (d. 748/1348)
4. *al-Bidāyah wa al-Nihāyah* ('The Beginning and the End') of Ibn Kathīr (d. 774/1373)

I also said: You should know that the books of history are filled with defects and corruption so be wary of them, as the eminent scholar Ibn Khaldūn noted:

> The pioneering Muslim historians made exhaustive collections of historical events and wrote them down in book form. But, then, persons who had no right to occupy themselves with history introduced into those books untrue gossip which they had thought up or freely invented, as well as false, discredited reports which they had made up or embellished. Many of their successors followed in their steps and passed that information on to us as they had heard it. They did not look for, nor pay any attention to, the causes of events and conditions, nor did they eliminate or reject nonsensical stories.
>
> Little effort is being made to get at the truth. The critical eye, as a rule, is not sharp. Errors and unfounded assumptions are closely allied and familiar elements in historical information. Blind trust in tradition is an inherited trait in human beings. Occupation with the (scholarly) disciplines on the part of those who have no right is widespread. But the

---

[111] A universal history work from the dawn of humanity until the author's time that is considered a primary reference in the discipline of Muslim history due to its early authorship and the renowned status of Ṭabarī.

[112] A universal world history work extending from the beginning of humanity until the late 'Abbāsid era written by the noted historian and polymath.

[113] An abridgement of the previous work.

> pasture of stupidity is unwholesome for mankind. No one can stand up against the authority of truth, and the evil of falsehood is to be fought with enlightening speculation. The reporter merely dictates and passes on (the material). It takes critical insight to sort out the hidden truth: it takes knowledge to lay truth bare and polish it so that critical insight may be applied to it.[114]

They asked: Which books help us to understand philosophy and history? I replied: The Muqaddimah of Ibn Khaldūn (d. 808/1406), without dispute, and then the various writings of the eminent scholars Shiblī Nuʻmānī and Sayyid Sulaymān Nadwī concerning general history, the history of culture and civilization, and the philosophy of history.

The asked: What are the most important books on the history of the Islamic sciences? I replied: *Fajr al-islām*, *Ḍuḥā al-islām*, and *Ẓahr al-islām* of Aḥmad Amīn (d. 1373/1954),[115] duly noting the shortcomings and defects in them, which I will not stir up here.

Biography of Abū al-ʻIrfān Nadwī

They asked: From whom did you learn history? I replied: From more than one person, but the best of them in my estimation is our Mawlānā Abū al-ʻIrfān Nadwī, may God have mercy upon him.

They asked: Benefit us with his biography. I replied: He is the Shaykh, scholar, great philosopher, writer, historian Abū al-ʻIrfān Nadwī, son of the Shaykh and scholar Dīn Muḥammad of Jawnpūr, who was one of the rare intelligent men. Mawlānā Abū al-ʻIrfān learned from his father and attended the circles of the godly scholar and great preacher Mawlānā Abūbakr Muḥammad Shīth of Jawnpūr, from whom he benefited greatly. He also studied philosophy and logic with some of the specialists of rational sciences in the city of Allahabad. He attended the Dār al-ʻUlūm seminary of Deoband and then Nadwat al-ʻUlamāʼ, ultimately graduating from there. His teachers here included the great scholar Sayyid Sulaymān Nadwī, with whom he spent prolonged time and was particularly devoted to. He was widely read and

[114] Ibn Khaldūn, *Muqaddimah*. Translation taken from Franz Rosenthal.

[115] He was a brilliant Egyptian scholar and historian whose works include these three volumes on the history of Islamic culture.

delved into books of philosophy and kalām (scholastic theology). He fell in love with the books of Shaykh al-Islām Ibn Taymiyyah and Shāh Walīullah of Delhi.

He taught at Nadwah for a very long time (probably about 45 years), serving as its vice principal as well as principal. He was known for teaching the Shāh Walīullah's *Ḥujjatullāh al-Bālighah*. He surpassed his peers in Urdu, Persian and Arabic literature, history, philosophy, scholastic theology (kalām), and the practices of the early Muslims. He knew the views of various sects and religions with great recall. He had memorized many texts and verses in multiple languages. He possessed abundant information, awareness of various cultures, rare intelligence, and the ability to speak with unrivaled eloquence. He used to represent Nadwat al-'Ulamā' in the largest academic conferences and forums. He had no rival in India in the grasp of the history of Islamic sciences, ranks of scholars, and educational methodologies. He translated the book *al-Thaqāfah al-islāmiyah fī al-hind* ('Islamic Culture in India') of the eminent scholar 'Abd al-Ḥayy al-Ḥasanī into Urdu.

He died on the 7th of Rabī' al-Thānī 1409/1988 at the age of sixty-five. I was among those who accompanied his funeral procession from Lucknow to Jawnpūr, where he was buried. His funeral was attended by a large group of people from various parts of the country. His death greatly affected me to the point that the fear of death nearly killed me. I was not able to sleep at night for some time.

I learned from him clear rhetoric and aspects of logic and philosophy. I also learned from him the first volume of the tafsīr of Bayḍāwī and the history of Islamic sciences. I also benefited greatly from his assemblies.

They asked: What was his methodology of teaching? I replied: His knowledge was entirely in his memory, and he had complete command and mastery over it. He never taught us, for instance, logic, philosophy or the history of Islamic sciences from any book or notes. Instead, he would dictate all of that to us, with complete recall of information, events, and history. He was also excellent at drawing conclusions and implications, and had an amazing ability to connect effects and occurrences with their causes and rationale.

They asked: Did he treat you in any special way while you were with him? I replied: No, but I did learn from him many things outside of the classroom. I transcribed a treatise of Shāh Walīullah from Persian to Arabic on the principles of learning and education, and he reviewed it with me and corrected some mistakes. He treated all of his students alike, but perhaps our colleague Muḥammad Ḥashmatullāh Nadwī had a stronger connection with him on account of being his neighbor in residence. Or perhaps the closest to him was our other colleague Muḥammad ʿAbd al-Ḥayy Nadwī, to whom he would dictate lengthy articles which he would present in various scholarly forums and conferences. ʿAbd al-Ḥayy would write them in his beautiful handwriting and preserve them.

They asked: Please mention some of the virtues of his piety or character. I replied: He was pure and protected from the ill motives of the heart, never being affected by envy or jealousy. He was kind and mild-mannered, pleasant towards his companions and students, and had many other good qualities.

He was the director of the kitchen at Nadwah and loved to eat. His love for tasty foods was the cause of his health problems, which included diabetes and heart attacks. Despite that, he was prone to sitting with people and telling jokes and witty anecdotes.

They asked: Tell us some of his funny moments. I replied: They are numerous, but I do remember once when he was sitting in the company of our Shaykh Abū al-Ḥasan ʿAlī Nadwī when some fine drink was brought to the assembly. Our Mawlānā Abū al-ʿIrfān took two glasses while everyone else had taken one. When asked why, he replied, "To the man is a portion equal to that of two females."[116]

---

[116] Taken from the Qur'ān 4:11, which references a specific scenario within the rules of inheritance. Though misunderstood as a general rule in inheritance law—which is certainly not the case as many scenarios have female relatives receiving more than male ones—what it means is that, with all other things being equal, males receive double the portion of females due to the burden of financial responsibility which Islam does not place upon females. In other words, males are legally obliged to spend upon their female dependents what they receive from all sources, including inheritance, while females can keep their shares entirely to themselves. In this way, as Shaykh Akram often points out, females are usually more privileged than males under the Sharīʿah since they are legally entitled to their own exclusive shares plus they are additionally entitled to the shares that their male relatives receive.

19

WHO TAUGHT YOU PRE-ISLAMIC POETRY

They asked: What is pre-Islamic poetry? I replied: It is poetry from the era of jāhiliyyah, which is the period of time immediately predating the Prophetic mission and spanning approximately one-and-a-half to two centuries. During this period, what we know now as pre-Islamic poetry was born. Al-Jāḥiẓ (d. 255/858-9) says in Kitāb al-Ḥaywān: "As for Arabic poetry, any discussion of its origins reveals that it is fairly young. The first to adopt its course and manner was Imra' al-Qays b. Ḥujr and Muhalhal b. Rabī'ah. When we review the whole of Arabic poetry—until the advent of Islam—we would find that it spans one hundred and fifty years, and if we were to review it even closer, then perhaps two hundred."

They asked: What are its most important sources? I replied: The registers[117] of poets and tribes; books of language and grammar; literature; books on history, biographies, and battles; and compilations of poetry—like the seven and the ten hanging odes (mu'allaqāt)[118], the Mufaḍḍaliyyāt,[119] al-Aṣma'iyyāt,[120] dīwān al-ḥamāsah works,[121] and *Jamharat ash'ār al-'arab* of Abū Zayd al-Qurashī.

They asked: What are their aims? I replied: Some of the most important themes they speak of include descriptives, praise, boasting, eulogies, invective, romance, lineage, wine, abstinence, wisdom, generosity, hosting guests, and other virtues. Pre-Islamic poetry became uniform upon one

---

[117] Singular *dīwān,* plural *dawāwīn.*

[118] *Mu'allaqāt,* literally 'hung poems,' refers to pre-Islamic Arabic verses or verse collections written in gold letters and hung on the walls of the Ka'bah in Makkah during annual fairs. They consist of seven (in some versions ten) odes, by different poets of the 6th century. They are generally regarded as the finest Arabic odes and present a lively picture of Bedouin life before Islam. (entry taken from *Madrasah Life.* London, UK: Turath Publishing. 2007.)

[119] An anthology of Arabic poems compiled by al-Mufaḍḍal al-Ḍabbī, an Ummayyad-then-'Abbāssid era linguist who died around 178/794.

[120] Compilation of Abū Sa'īd al-Aṣma'ī, a celebrated 'Abbāsid-era grammarian of the Baṣran school who frequented the court of Hārūn al-Rashīd. He died in 216/831.

[121] The ḥamāsah (literally, "valour") is a genre of Arabic poetry that recounts chivalrous exploits in the context of military glories and victories. The earliest and most famous is one by Abū Tamīm (see next chapter).

particular group of pattern and meter, and rarely departed from that. Authors would often begin by standing at ruins, weeping over buildings, and then describe their journeys, camels, horses, deserts, and sing about beautiful and harsh natures. They would move on to the real aims for which the ode was compiled. Some poets even expressed their boredom with this way of opening. ʿAntarah, for instance, states:

Is anything unsung by poets? What to say? Love, comes to me.
After thinking deeply, the abode of your beloved, can you see?[122]

Kaʿb b. Zuhayr says:

We find ourselves speaking borrowed words
Or returning to our own, over and over

Benefits of Learning Pre-Islamic Poetry

They asked: What is the benefit of studying this poetry? I replied: It has two major benefits.

First, from the study of pre-Islamic poetry we learn of ancient Arab culture and civilization. It was said long ago, "Poetry represents the registers of the Arabs." It envisages their social, religious, political and intellectual life, and their manners and inclinations. It also helps us understand many verses of the Qur'ān which expose, repudiate and correct the beliefs, practices, and customs of the pre-Islamic Arabs.

Second, we rely on this poetry in order to understand the language and modes of expression of the Qur'ān, for it was revealed in the language and expressions of those very people. Poetry represents the registers and storehouses of that language. Through this poetry, we can understand the ways and manners of their speaking and expression, and arrive at the meanings and implications of words and speech. ʿAbdullah b. ʿAbbās said, "If any words of the Qur'ān are obscure to you, then seek their meanings from poetry, for it represents the register of the Arabs."[123] Ibn ʿAbbās would often

---

[122] Sells, Michael A. *Desert Tracings: Six Classic Arabian Odes.* Connecticut, USA: Wesleyan University Press. 1989.

[123] Related by Bayhaqī al-Asmā' wa al-Ṣifāt and al-Ḥākim in al-Mustadrak.

answer questions about the Qur'ān by citing poetry. ʿUmar b. al-Khaṭṭāb said, "People, hold on to the register of your poetry from your pre-Islamic days, for within lies the interpretation of your Book."[124]

Muḥammad Rābiʿ Nadwī's Manner of Teaching Poetry

They asked: Who taught you pre-Islamic poetry? I replied: Mawlānā Muḥammad Rābiʿ Ḥasanī Nadwī, whose biography has already been mentioned.

They asked: How did he explain pre-Islamic poetry? I replied: He built his explanations upon the following points:

1. He would speak in detail about the era: the land, geography, tribes, and their values and characteristics.
2. He would elaborate on the poet himself: his origins, environment and interests.
3. He would discuss the ode itself: its poetical goals and aims, and their connection with its content.
4. He would analyze the verses from a linguistic and literary perspective: clarifying the meaning of difficult terms, morphology of specific words, the methodology of the poet in connecting his ideas, and demonstrating his views through each couplet.
5. In the end of each ode, he would summarize in his own unique way the central notions of the ode, trace its influence in Arab culture, and on readers in general.

They asked: You mentioned the purity and piety of the shaykh, so how would he explain the lines of the Muʿallaqah of Imraʾ al-Qays that were more depraved and licentious? I replied: He was bashful and noble during his teaching, so he would not explain those lines but skip over them and tell us to look up their explanations ourselves.

[124] Quoted by Shāṭibī in al-Muwāfaqāt, but no strong isnād exists elsewhere.

20

WHO TAUGHT YOU POETRY AND PROSE

They asked: What is the best compilation of poetry? I replied: *Dīwān al-Ḥamāsah* of Abū Tamām Ḥabīb b. Aws b. al-Ḥārith al-Ṭā'ī (d. 231/845). He was born in Jāsim, Syria. After being summoned by the 'Abbāssid Caliph al-Mu'taṣim to Baghdad, he praised the Caliph with moving verses and was admitted into his court among the other poets. His selection of poetry is known as al-Ḥamasah in accordance with his practice of naming each section after the beginning of its contents. The first chapter (and the entire collection) is named al-ḥamāsah (valour), while the subsequent chapters are named as follows: marāthī (elegies), adab (conduct), nasīb (love), hijā' (invective), aḍyāf wa madīḥ (hospitality and praise), ṣifāt (descriptions), sayr wa nu'ās (desert travel), mulaḥ (anecdotes), and madhammat al-nisā' (censure of women). He chose from a wide array of well-known and reputable poetry from pre-Islamic and Islamic periods, including Ummayad-era selections, and even contemporary 'Abbāssid-era ones to some extent.

They asked: What are its most important commentaries? I replied: There are two: that of Aḥmad b. Muḥammad al-Marzūqī and Abū Zakariyyā Yaḥyā b. 'Alī al-Khaṭīb al-Tabrīzī, both of which have been published and are widely circulated.

They asked: Can you make us more familiar with this dīwān? I replied: It became famous from the moment it was authored by Abū Tamām and widely accepted by scholars and people of letters. It was unrivalled among compilations and registers of poetry, for it contained the very best of what was compiled by poets up until that point, and the author confined himself to shorter poems. The work testifies to the full extent of Abū Tamām's competence and expertise in recognizing the merits of poetry. He only included the finest, most eloquent, and best-composed verses which spoke of noble ethics and lofty aspirations.

Biography of Shafīq al-Raḥmān Nadwī

They asked: Who taught you that compilation? I replied: Our teacher Mawlānā Shafīq al-Raḥmān Nadwī.

They said: Please provide us his biography. I replied: He was the scholar, man of letters and jurist Shafīq al-Raḥmān Nadwī, who was born in Jimbaran in the Indian state of Bihār in 1361/1942. He studied at the Islamic University of Bettiah and other institutions before joining Nadwat al-ʿUlamāʾ where he surpassed his peers and graduated in 1380/1960.

He taught in various places and was ultimately appointed at the Nadwah in 1392/1972, where he fulfilled his duties diligently. He was proficient in Urdu and Arabic, and authored *al-Fiqh al-Muyassar* ("Fiqh Made Easy") in Ḥanafī jurisprudence.

I read to him Dīwān al-Ḥamāsah and learned from him Arabic composition and writing for about a year. He died on the thirteenth of Rabīʿ al-Thānī in 1423/2002.

They asked: What are the best compilations of prose? I replied: The 2-volume *Mukhtārāt min adab al-ʿarab* of our Shaykh Abū al-Ḥasan ʿAlī Nadwī.

They asked: Describe it for us. I replied: This two-volume work consists of seventy-three literary texts representing the best of Arabo-Islamic composition in all its manifestations in various fields—literary, historic and cultural—dating from the first Islamic period to the fourteenth Ḥijrī century. It also includes the best examples of various types of Arabic composition, from heavenly revelation and Prophetic eloquence to speeches of the most famous Arab speakers from the golden periods, and many narrations, stories, letters and portions of books. It also includes debates, discussions, travelogues, and even simple domestic conversations. It includes the serious and light-hearted, wise sayings, and jest. It expands the readers' horizons of thought and expression, takes his mind on a flight through the real and imagined, and entices him to enjoy the beauty of the Arabic language.

This book, along with its innovative introduction, is considered a revolution in thinking and an extraordinary endeavor in the domain of literature. Great Arab litterateurs have recognized his merit in opening a new direction in the already vast field of Islamic literature. He flipped the literary scales and crossed traditional boundaries set by litterateurs blindly following the contours of literature for centuries. This book became a new nucleus and foundation that established the bounds of a sounder Islamic literary tradition.

The great man of letters Shaykh ʿAlī Ṭanṭāwī said:

> If it is true that the selections of a literary scholar prove his taste in literature, then it suffices readers to know that a short while ago, we selected one book out of many literary collections and place it now in the hands of students of advanced Sharīʿah studies in Syria. Every single member of the committee—each a literary scholar in his own right—after researching and investigating the matter, arrived at the same conclusion: that the best and most comprehensive book on the art of expression is the *Mukhtārāt* of Shaykh Abū al-Ḥasan.
>
> I used to think for a long time about ways to escape, with our students, from the dark and tight prison we had placed them in, to come out into the air of freedom and the light of day. We should not have limited our selections to *Waṣf al-Kitāb* of al-Jāḥiẓ—which is composed of seemingly related sentences without any overarching theme tying them or providing life or spirit—or to the pastimes of Ibn al-ʿAmīd,[125] the viscious discourses of al-Ṣāḥib,[126] or the technicalities of al-Qāḍī al-Fāḍil.[127] These selections often cause students to despise literature. We would tell them that truthful expression lies elsewhere, that Abū Ḥayyān al-Tawḥīdī[128] was more versed than al-Jāḥiẓ though al-Jāḥiẓ was more prolific, famed and trained in the sciences and arts of expression, and that Ḥasan

[125] Minister to the first ruler of the Shīʿite Buwayhid/Buyyid dynasty Rukn al-Dawlah, Abū al-Faḍl Muḥammad b. al-Ḥusayn (d. 360) was a writer and philosopher praised by Mutanabbī and known as "the second Jāḥiẓ." It was said that writing began with ʿAbd al-Ḥamīd and ended with Ibn al-ʿAmīd.

[126] Minister to the second Buwayhid ruler Muʾayyad al-Dawlah son of Rukn al-Dawla, his name was Abū al-Qāsim Ismāʿīl b. ʿAbbād, better known as al-Ṣāḥib ("the Companion") due his being a companion of Ibn al-ʿAmīd. He was Shīʿite in beliefs and known for his harsh views towards Sunnīs. He died in 385.

[127] Great scholar and linguist who was born in Aschelon, Palestine in 529 and later settled in Egypt, where he served as a minister to Ṣalāḥ al-Dīn Ayyūbī. The great ruler Ṣalāḥ al-Dīn said of him "Don't think that I conquered these lands with your swords, but it was with the pen of al-Qāḍī al-Fāḍil." He died in Cairo in 596/1200.

[128] He was a writer and philosopher of Baghdad deemed heretical by Sunnī scholars such as Dhahabī and Ibn al-Jawzī. He died in 414/1023.

al-Baṣrī (d. 110/728) was more rhetorically eloquent than both, and that Ibn al-Simāk (d. 183) was even more so.

On the other hand, it is far better and more beneficial from a literary perspective for students to look to Ghazālī's *Iḥyā' 'Ulūm al-Dīn*, Ibn Khaldūn's *Muqaddimah*, Ibn al-Jawzī's *Ṣayd al-Khāṭir*, Ibn Hishām's Sīrah, Shāfi'ī's *al-Umm*, and Sarakhsī's *Mabsūṭ*, than the foolish ramblings of al-Ṣāḥib or the prattle of al-Ḥarīrī or Ibn al-Athīr.

I wrote about these matters a number of times but found no ears, to my dismay, until I discovered the book of Abū al-Ḥasan, which had shaken the books of the literary and historical tradition, extracted their jewels, and deposited them into his work.

I do not claim to have originated this thinking, or to suggest that he borrowed it from me. Rather, it is more likely that he never read any of my writings nor anyone else's on this issue. What drove him was his sharp literary taste and authentic Arab temperament.[129]

Biography of Shams al-Ḥaqq Nadwī

They asked: Who taught you this book? I replied: Our teacher Mawlānā Shams al-Ḥaqq Nadwī.

They said: Please provide us with his biography. I replied: He was the literary scholar and esteemed journalist Mawlānā Shams al-Ḥaqq Nadwī, born in 1357/1939 in Yaḥyāpūr in Burtābakrāh. He learned Persian in his hometown and Arabic in the Bāqiyat al-'Ulūm school. He joined Nadwat al-'Ulamā' in 1373/1954. He learned Qur'ānic exegesis from Mawlānā Muḥammad Uways Najrāmī Nadwī; geography of Arabia from our Mawlānā Muḥammad Rābi' Ḥasanī Nadwī; Riyāḍ al-Ṣāliḥīn from Mawlānā Mu'īnullāh Nadwī; the books al-Hidāyah, Mishkāt al-Maṣābīḥ and Nukhbat al-Fikr from Mawlānā Muḥammad Asbāṭ; Arabic rhetoric from our Mawlānā Abū al-'Irfān Nadwī; Sunan Tirmidhī from Mawlānā Muḥammad Manẓūr Nu'mānī; the Book of Knowledge from Ṣaḥīḥ Bukhārī from our Shaykh Abū al-Ḥasan; all of

[129] Pg. 5. Shaykh Abū al-Ḥasan 'Alī Nadwī, *Mukhtārāt Min Adab al-'Arab*. Damascus, Syria: Dār Ibn al-Kathīr. 1420/1999. Also from pg. 17-8. *Al-Muslimūn fī al-Hind*. Damascus, Syria: Dār Ibn al-Kathīr. 1420/1999.

Ṣaḥīḥ Bukhārī from Mawlānā Muḥammad Isḥāq Sandailwī and Mawlānā Muḥammad Ayyūb A'ẓamī Mi'awī; Muwaṭṭa', Ṣaḥīḥ Muslim and Sunan Abū Dāwūd from Mawlānā Muḥammad Isḥāq Sandailwī and Mawlānā 'Abd al-Ḥafīẓ Bilyāwī; and Tafsīr Bayḍāwī from Mawlānā 'Abd al-Ḥafīẓ Bilyāwī.

He graduated from Nadwah in November 1382/1962 and immediately became a teacher along with being head of publication for the Urdu newspaper Ta'mīr-e Ḥayāt published at Nadwah. He was one of the closest people to our Shaykh Abū al-Ḥasan and also enjoyed the confidence of our Mawlānā Muḥammad Rābi' Ḥasanī Nadwī. He was also the author of a number of works.

He was distinguished by his good character, humility, nobility, softness, love, purity, and avoidance of anything that would harm the honor of others and all vain pastimes. He was always joyful, cheerful and smiling.

I learned from him *Mukhtārāt Min Adab al-'Arab,* Arabic composition, and Arabic speaking.

21

WHO TAUGHT YOU MEDIA AND COMMUNICATION

They asked: What exactly is the subject of media and communication (iʿlām)? I replied: It is basically the dissemination of news and information, but the term is also used for all the means and resources associated with that process. Moreover, it has now exceeded that conventional meaning to encroach upon the roles of cultural programming, general education, moral instruction, recreation and entertainment, and even marketing and stimulation. Today, it is one of the greatest mediums to connect with the masses, inform of events and occurrences, and to exchange views, feelings and emotions among humankind. It also promotes insidious propaganda, persistent falsehoods, shameful aberrations and all sorts of fabrications and untruths on behalf of nation-states, agencies, corporations, political groups and other associations.

They asked: What do you mean by the means and resources associated with the dissemination of news? I replied: They include print resources like newspapers, magazines and journals; audio-visual resources like radio and television; electronic media; and various forms of social media. This last type (social media) has brought about a startling leap and great revolution in the world of communication, as it has freed media from the grip of state-control and politics, and from the influence of various agencies and their competing interests.

They asked: What is the power of media? I replied: No person can deny the extent of influence and power of media upon individual persons and societies. It is far more effective and has greater reach than systematic education. It is a global invention not bound by borders and lines. It has ravaged cities, villages and rural areas alike—even deserts and caves, seas and oceans. It is a matter of great interest to developed nations, which have allocated huge budgets and great manpower to focus on the development of technical tools and devices that would be easy to be acquired by every home, office, agency and individual. In effect, they have provided water to people who weren't thirsty, forcing them to enjoy it and toying with their mind and thought.

They said: It pains us to see the media being used for negative goals. I replied: Its main purpose is to communicate among people by relaying information, news, opinions and trends, but it was greatly misused which wound up revealing its hidden secret. It now promotes negative goals, malicious intentions, and destructive movements. It spreads aberrant ideas, lewd images, deviant behavior, and tears down conventional covers and barriers in order to dilute and destroy society. Its usage for evil, corruption, and harm is far greater than its use for good and reform, or for rectification, building and redeeming actions. It is as if social media and corruption were in unholy wedlock with no way out. You now find people thirsty for it like people craving cold water on hot blazing days and desperate camels clambering for a spot at a watering hole. All of that is the result of humanity's transgression—moving away from its pure innate nature, sound intellect and from faith; and its rebellion against noble values, ideals and ethics. In this scheme, even teachers and educators have become weak-minded and dull.

They asked: What is the best way to protect ourselves from the negative effects of media? I replied: The cultural-intellectual war for which media has been appropriated must elicit a strong sense of repulsion and repudiation coupled with a spirit of resistance and opposition within the hearts and minds of morally-minded individuals concerned with education and learning. It would surely be a grave sin and crime were we to feebly stand before this state of affairs in surrender and weakness. This media war is no less important than any military war. In fact, it is far more deadly and destructive. In addition, there is no way to challenge it other than returning to the fundamental source of guidance— the Qur'ān, and its rightly guided teacher—the Seal of the Prophets, along with relying on these two sources for the purification of one's heart and soul.

He who purifies it will prosper,
and he who suppresses it will be ruined.[130]

[130] Qur'ān 91:9-10.

Biography of Nadhr al-Ḥafīẓ Nadwī

They asked: From whom did you learn the subject of media at Nadwat al-'Ulamā'? I replied: From our teacher the eminent scholar Mawlānā Nadhr al-Ḥafīẓ Nadwī, author of the widely known work, *Al-I'lām al-Gharbī wa Ta'thīratuhū 'alā al-Mujtama'* ("Western Media and its Effects on Society"), which is unique in its topic.

They said: Provide us with his biography. I replied: He is our pious and devout teacher, scholar, linguist and distinguished journalist Mawlānā Nadhr al-Ḥafīẓ b. 'Abd al-Ḥafīẓ b. Muḥammad Isḥāq b. Khudā Bakhsh Abū Mu'ẓam Nadwī Azharī. He was born in 1358/1939 in the village of Mulmul, district of Madhubani, in the Indian state of Bihār. His maternal grandfather was Mawlānā Sirāj al-Dīn a graduate of the Maẓāhir al-'Ulūm school and one of the spiritual successors of Ashraf 'Alī Thānwī.

He memorized the Qur'ān in the Kāfiyat al-'Ulūm school in Burtābakrāh where his father was a teacher and close companion of the pious scholar and teacher Mawlānā Muḥammad Aḥmad Burtābakdhī. Mawlānā Nadhr al-Ḥafīẓ also learned in that school Urdu and Persian, as well as the Gulistān and Bustān of Mawlānā Shīrāzī Sa'dī from his uncle Mawlānā Muḥammad 'Āqil. He became proficient in Persian to the extent that he would correspond with his father in the language.

He joined Nadwat al-'Ulamā' in 1374/1954, earned his 'ālimiyyah degree by 1381/1961, and the faḍīlah specialization two years after that. He learned the Muwaṭṭa' through the transmission of Yaḥyā b. Yaḥyā al-Laythī from Mawlānā Muḥammad Asbāṭ; some portions from the beginning of Ṣaḥīḥ Bukhārī from our Shaykh Abū al-Ḥasan 'Alī Nadwī; the entirety of Ṣaḥīḥ Bukhārī from the ḥadīth scholar Mawlānā Muḥammad Ayyūb A'ẓamī; Ṣaḥīḥ Muslim, Sunan al-Nasā'ī and Sunan Ibn Mājah from the great and eminent scholar Mawlānā Muḥammad Isḥāq Sandhelwī; Sunan Tirmidhī from the eminent scholar Mawlānā Muḥammad Manẓūr Nu'mānī; Mishkāt al-Maṣabīḥ from Mawlānā Muḥammad Asbāṭ and Mawlānā Wajīh al-Dīn Nadwī; Hidāyat al-Fiqh from our teacher Mawlānā Muḥammad Ẓahūr Nadwī; and Arabic literature from our two teachers Mawlānā Muḥammad Rābi' Nadwī and Mawlānā Sa'īd al-Raḥmān A'ẓamī. He was granted a general ijāzah from Mawlānā Abū al-Ḥasan 'Alī Nadwī.

He joined al-Azhar University in 1394/1974 and earned a masters in literature and literary critique. His dissertation was on Zamakhsharī as a writer and poet.

He taught at al-Rashād University in Azamgarh and then at Nadwah. He was most known for his journalistic skills. He wrote some powerful pieces for the Nidā' al-Millah newspaper in Lucknow as well as other periodicals. He was also one of the strongest teachers at Nadwah in language and literature. He is currently the dean of the College of Arabic Language and Literature. One of his most famous works is *Abū al-Ḥasan al-Nadwī Kātiban wa Mufakkiran* ("Abū al-Ḥasan Nadwī, the Writer, the Thinker").[131]

I learned media studies from him, as well as heresiology and contemporary Islamic world affairs. He is one of my pious and sincere teachers, who fills the hearts of his students and colleagues with his upright, mature and praiseworthy manner and his refined conduct in all circumstances.

They asked: What would you advise us concerning the subject of media? I replied: The issue of media is grave and serious. We must understand its importance and study all of its dimensions. We must strive to save it from corruption and immorality, and seek instead to make media a positive force and a promoter of morality and virtue. We must present this purified media to the future, and use it in the service of knowledge, religion, and the promotion of noble values, ideals and ethics. We must use to it protect human souls from all that would tarnish it. This is a difficult task for those who are liberal-minded. We ask God to protect us from all immorality, open and hidden.

---

[131] Nadwī, Nadhr al-Ḥafīẓ. *Abū al-Ḥasan al-Nadwī kātiban wa mufakkiran*. Kuwait: Dār al-Nashr wa al-Tawzī'. 1407/1986.

❁22❁

WHO TAUGHT YOU LITERARY TASTE

They asked: What exactly is literary taste? I replied: It is a faculty that enables a person to look at literary work and artistic creation and appreciate what is good from what is defective, beautiful from ugly, and truly enjoyable from abhorrent. It allows the reader of literary texts, onlooker of works of art, and listener of verses of poetry, for instance, to find what is pleasing and enjoyable, and learn what causes distaste and repulsion. What makes all this possible is nothing but a literary or artistic sense which is built upon a certain amount of prerequisite knowledge and sound understanding, for literary taste is not only emotionally-based but also a rational and academic process.

They asked: What is its role in literary criticism? I replied: Literary taste creates the capacity to distinguish between merit and weakness, and the resulting ability to judge the beauty and ugliness of texts and to reveal their distinctions and flaws from the perspective of rhetorical and expressive power. So literary taste has a fundamental role in evaluation and judgement based upon a serious study and academic-literary analysis of texts. There is no consideration for anything here except the literary taste of experts, as is the case with all disciplines and crafts which are the domain of their own respective leaders of experience and expertise. How many times have we seen scholars who are Indian and non-Arab deem the most graceful and esteemed verses of poetry as ugly and distasteful, or judge poorly composed and ill words as splendid and eloquent? This, in fact, represents nothing but a lack of literary taste and instinct in the Arabic language.

They asked: What are the ways to increase this instinct? I replied: The basis for it is an innate readiness that already exists within, which alone is not enough to attain this literary instinct but must be developed further by various means. These include expanding one's cultural horizons, interaction with experts and critics of literature and poetry, and reading the best examples of brilliant, captivating compositions and beautiful enchanting texts. They also include understanding the secrets of language, attaining proficiency in the principles of grammar, morphology and rhetorical eloquence, and the reading of the creative works of great poets and writers with full understanding and enjoyment. This is the proper way to establish that instinct and ability, which can be supported and strengthened even further by the study of psychology, sociology and aesthetics.

Ibn Khaldūn states in the Muqaddimah:

> The word 'taste' is in current use among those who are concerned with the various branches of literary criticism. It means the tongue's possession of the habit of eloquence. . . An eloquent speaker of the Arabic language chooses the form (of expression) that affords such conformity according to the methods and ways of Arab address. In this respect he hardly ever sways from the way of Arab eloquence.
>
> Habits that are firmly established and rooted in their proper places appear to be natural and innate in those places. Therefore, many ignorant people who are not acquainted with the importance of habits, think that the correct use of vowel endings and the proper eloquence of Arabs in their language are natural things. They say that 'the Arabs speak (correct Arabic) by nature.' This is not so. Correct Arabic speech) is a linguistic habit of (proper) speech arrangement that has become firmly established and rooted (in speakers of Arabic), so that, superficially, it appears to be something natural and innate. However, as mentioned before, this habit results from the constant practice of Arabic speech and from repeated listening to it and from understanding the peculiar qualities of its word combinations. It is not obtained through knowledge of the scientific rules evolved by literary critics. Those rules merely afford a knowledge of the Arabic language. They do not give (a person) possession of the actual habit in its proper place.[132]

Biography of ʿAbd al-Nūr Nadwī

They asked: From which of your teachers did you learn this literary sense? I replied: I learned it from my teacher Mawlānā 'Abd al-Nūr Nadwī. They said:

[132] Pg. 439-40. Ibn Khaldūn. The Muqaddimah: An Introduction to History. Translated by Franz Rosenthal. New Jersey, US: Princeton University Press. 2005.

Provide us his biography. I replied: He is our teacher, the man of letters, possessor of great literary sense, both natural and acquired, the esteemed scholar Mawlānā 'Abd al-Nūr b. 'Abd al-'Aẓīm Nadwī Azharī, better known as Mawlānā Nūr 'Aẓīm Nadwī. He graduated first from Nadwat al-'Ulamā' and later from al-Azhar University. His master's dissertation was on the "reality of literary taste, its means for development and its role in literary critique."

He taught at Nadwah as well as Dār al-'Ulūm al-Aḥmadiyyah al-Salafiyyah and headed the journal al-Hudā. He also taught at Imām Muḥammad b. Sa'ūd Islamic University in the Institute for the Teaching of Arabic to Non-Native Speakers, and later returned to Nadwah to serve the remaining years of his life in service to our Shaykh Abū al-Ḥasan 'Alī Nadwī, Mawlānā Muḥammad Rābi' Ḥasanī Nadwī, and the students of the institution.

He was one of the premier scholars of Arabic and Urdu literature in the Indian subcontinent. He was not a litterateur who took a bit of everything in order to lose himself or his identity, but he was one who took literature from all sides to become proficient in the full breadth of its universe and to defend its valuable treasures. He was distinguished from his peers by his rare and experienced literary sense and expertise in all its dimensions. He also had a keen ability to transfer that literary sense to his students and colleagues. He was known in intellectual and literary circles for his extensive and detailed journalistic experience, and his own practice in the vocation of journalism was characterized by integrity, freedom, a sense of Prophetic mission, and service to people and nations. He possessed a rare ability to organize and manage scholarly seminars in a self-confident and wonderfully spontaneous way. He was known for tolerance and flexibility in jurisprudential matters, even as he was a follower of the early predecessors. In fact, he rarely professed any jurisprudential or theological affiliation. In that, he exemplified the way of Nadwat al-'Ulamā' in rising above debates in subsidiary matters and arguments which lead to hatred, hostility and conflict. How painful it is to see the return of this abhorrent sectarianism among scholars and students, may God never bless that!

I learned from him psychology, sociology, aesthetics, and much in the way of literary and journalistic matters. He would proofread my articles and translations, point out the errors and mistakes contained therein and help refine my style of presentation. In that, he was at once a loving father, a sincere and truthful teacher, and a skilled and proficient expert.

He died on the 8th of Sha'bān on 1413/1993, leaving a massive intellectual and cultural void at Nadwah. I cannot ever envision that institution without his towering personality.

He was gone far too soon, but his achievements during his short life of literary writings and the raising of a generation of young people suffice in attesting to his merits:

About a person do not ask but instead about his associates
For every associate does emulate his peers[133]

Perhaps he was second to our Mawlānā Muḥammad Wāḍiḥ Rashīd Nadwī in teaching and training students in writing, especially in the Urdu language. Students loved and respected him greatly. I could not count how many times we would go to his house to learn from him, read to him and drink from his pure spring of knowledge. He was never miserly with us nor did he ever hold back. Instead, he was noble, generous and lenient with us. He was refined, gentle-natured, pure in speech and writing, and keen in perception. He possessed so many rare intellectual and literary insights that those in his company would never get tired or bored.

133 Mu'allaqah Ṭarafah b. al-'Abd.

❁23❁

WHO TAUGHT YOU LITERARY CRITICISM

They asked: What is literary criticism? I replied: It is the study of literary works and all it entails—interpretation, detailed investigation; comparative analysis; highlighting of merits, flaws, strengths, and weaknesses; and uncovering style and beauty. It is, in other words, providing an accurate assessment of a literary text by revealing its real value and rank, and analyzing its stylistic peculiarity.

They asked: What is stylistic peculiarity, and how do you analyze it? I replied: Stylistic peculiarity is the specific path that a writer or scholar pursues in order to render a meaning from a range of possible meanings. Its analysis consists of studying all of its components separately (each by itself) and collectively (all of the elements in unison).

They asked: What are these elements? I replied: They are four basic principles and pillars of a literary work: idea, sentiment, imagination, and form.

They asked: Can you explain each of these? I replied: An idea is what occurs in the mind of the author to work towards refining, coordinating and ordering meanings. The idea emanates from the author's attitudes towards life and all its human manifestations, both natural and synthetic.

Sentiment, or passion, refers to the author's psychological awareness or sense. He sees something which overtakes him and elicits some sort of response, like pleasure or anger, love or hatred, joy or sadness, a sense of security or fear, or any myriad human emotions. Passion depends upon a sense of concordance, stirring up feelings and emotions, and patterns of coherence and harmony.

Imagination is a talent by which the author envisions or visualizes that which concerns him by relying on his specific experiences and using techniques of analogy, similitude, metaphor, allegory, and allusion.

Verbal form is a garment composed of words and expressions for the purposes of a literary work, through which it is possible for the listener or reader to effect or actualize its meaning and realities. It is comprised of words, sentences, and phrases of a language and all that is related in terms of literal expression or formal rendition.

Biography of Sa'īd al-Raḥmān A'ẓamī Nadwī

They asked: From whom did you learn this? I replied: I learned it from our teacher Mawlānā Sa'īd al-Raḥmān A'ẓamī, the head of Nadwah, through his teaching of Islamic poetry and the book *al-Adab al-'Arabī bayna 'Araḍ wa al-Naqd* ('Arabic Literature between Presenting and Critiquing') by Mawlānā Muḥammad Rābi' Ḥasanī Nadwī.

They asked: What is this book? I replied: It is a book that discusses the reality of literature, analysis and critique of literary texts, and presents examples of Arabic literature from various periods with explanations of their artistic value. Professor Aḥmad al-Jundī said about it "Indeed this book in its small size is considered a significant service for literature students in foreign lands, and a beneficial summary of our literature. It deserves every appraisal and admiration." Our Shaykh Abū al-Ḥasan 'Alī Nadwī said: "Being fully cognizant of this benevolence, and with great delight and renewed joy, I present this book that meets a need and fills a gap in the teaching of the Arabic language and Arabic literature in India. . . . It is a book that combines literary texts with a glimpse of the history of Arabic literature and its various stages; and that all the trends, currents, events and factors which faced it and imparted on it a new color."

They said: Give us the biography of your teacher. I replied: He was the ingenious learned scholar, witty man of letters, and intelligent public speaker, Sa'īd al-Raḥmān A'ẓamī Nadwī b. Mawlānā Ayyūb b. Mawlānā Muḥammad Ṣābir b. Mawlānā Muḥammad Jīwah, from the village of Bakhtawar Ganj in the city of Mau.

His father Ayyūb A'ẓamī was a great scholar—whom I had the good fortune to visit—who was from the students of the eminent scholar Anwar Shāh Kashmīrī. He graduated from Dār al-'Ulūm Deoband in 1338/1919. He taught at the Miftāḥ al-'Ulūm school of Mau and worked as teacher of ḥadīth at Ta'līm al-Dīn school in Dabhel.

Mawlānā Sa'īd al-Raḥmān A'ẓamī was born on the fourteenth of May 1353/1934 (his certificate mistakenly mentioned 1936). He learned from his father Mishkāt al-Maṣābīḥ, Ṣaḥīḥ Muslim, al-Hidāya, and the summary of al-Ma'ānī in the Miftāḥ al-'Ulūm school of Mau. He also learned the six ḥadīth books from the great ḥadīth scholar Mawlānā Ḥabīb al-Raḥmān Aʿẓamī and received ijāzah from him. He also received ijāzah in the musalsal[134] ḥadīth works and other things from Mawlānā Muḥammad Zakariyyā Kandihlawī, the eminent scholar Taqī al-Dīn Hilālī (from whom he also learned Arabic literature, writing and literary instinct), Shaykh Abū al-Ḥasan ʿAlī Nadwī and Shaykh ʿAbd al-Fattāḥ Abū Ghuddah.

I read to him *al-adab al-ʿArabī bayna ʿaraḍ wa al-naqd* of Mawlānā Muḥammad Rābiʿ Ḥasanī Nadwī, selections from the Diwān of Hassān b. Thābit al-Anṣārī, and *Madhā khasira al-ʿālam bi inḥiṭāṭ al-muslimīn* of Shaykh Abū al-Ḥasan. I also learned from him Arabic composition and writing, and he wrote me a general ijazah on the 25th Jamādī al-Ūlā in the year 1422/2001. He had several excellent literary and Islamic writings that indicate the depth of his research, strength of argument, eloquence of style, and wonderful presentation.

They said: Mention to us of his merits. I replied: He was a model for the world of Nadwah: zealous in faith, guarding of nobility, and composed of behavior and outward appearance. He possessed a strong personality and behaved like a dignified father among his students. A manner of awe-inspiring calmness accompanied him in his appearance and speech. He preferred following precedent and despised innovating. Perhaps the most important of his merits are three:

First, there is his tireless activity, interconnected effort, hard-work, and diligence in the duties of teaching, leadership, speaking and management. He was punctual and maintained his appointments with full commitment. He was the first to enter the classroom and the last to leave, without being disruptive. He did not tolerate any drivel or disobedience. Whenever students saw him, they were overwhelmed by a cloud of composure, calm, and reverence. He always entered the mosque before the time of prayer and fulfilled his prayers on time. This was his perpetual habit, in the summer or winter, in times of strong wind, violent storms, pouring rain, and during floods or torrents.

His second merit was his speed in writing and spontaneous intuition in public speaking. He was greatly learned and intimately familiar with Arabic. He had a powerful and brilliant pen. His writing was fluent and impossible to imitate. He delivered sermons with an excited and resounding voice that

[134] See footnote 81.

reached into souls, and words flowed from his tongue in perfect proportion. In his writing and speaking, he was an avid reader of classical Arabic and despised slang or incorrect grammar. We are amazed at how the Shaykh, despite his preoccupations of teaching and management, was able to study, think, preach, and write. His speeches had a major role in driving the clouds of the Arabic language onto the courtyard of Nadwah and transforming it into to the markets of Ukādh, Majannah, and Dhū al-Majāz,[135] exhibiting the eloquence of Najd and the expressions of Arabia.

His third merit was his eagerness in benefitting students. Proof of that is that he would often teach us in his house outside of class hours at Nadwah. Students would read to him various literary and intellectual books, and he would correct their reading and pronunciation. He was extremely strict about correct and proper articulation, reading, and writing.

They asked: Did you attend his classes outside of his house? I replied: I only had the chance to do so once or twice, but the keenest of my companions to attend these lessons were Muḥammad Ḥashmatullāh Nadwī, Khālid Barkat ʿAlī, Ḍiyā' al-Dīn Aʿẓamī and a few others.

They asked: How did you benefit from him outside of teaching? I replied: I would often sit with him in the office of the periodical al-Baʿth al-Islāmī ('Islamic Research'), of which he was chief editor. He would appoint me to write for the periodical and published many of my articles and translations. He would also ask me to help in correcting some of the articles that were to be published in the magazine but were not at an appropriate level. I became close to him because my classmate and friend Muḥammad ʿAbd al-Ḥayy Nadwī was the head of the office of the periodical. I would often visit my friend there and wind up perusing the periodicals and Arabic journals, benefitting greatly. May God reward our noble teacher and repay him with more than he worked and strove for. May God bless his life and raise him to lofty ranks.

---

[135] These were three of the four well-known market-festivals of ancient Arabia where competitions between the best poets were held.

❁24❁

WHO TAUGHT YOU DIALECTICS

They asked: What is the art of dialectics (jadal)? I replied: For logicians, it is an analogical process composed of familiar assumptions and premises that necessitate certain deductions intended for those who fall short of understanding introductory evidences. For most other scholars, it refers to engaging in dialogue for the purpose of contesting or disputing something; to confront one proof with another, or one evidence for another; to review two matters for the sake of judging between them; or to refute or reject a statement or view.

They asked: What are its proper rules? I replied: Both sides must agree to uncover and reveal the truth, not hide it; and to rid the heart of any desire to overcome, dominate, belittle, or ridicule the opponent.

Biography of Nāṣir ʿAlī Nadwī

They asked: From whom did you learn dialectics? I replied: I learned from my teacher Mawlānā Nāṣir ʿAlī Nadwī. They asked: Tell us about him. I replied: He was the pious, learned and brilliant scholar, specialist of jurisprudence and its foundations, and of ḥadīth, Mawlānā Nāṣir ʿAlī b. ʿĀshiq ʿAlī Nadwī of Lucknow. He was born in 1354/1935 in Khurram Nagar in rural Lucknow. In 1367/1943, he joined Nadwah and graduated in 1376/1956. He learned from senior teachers such as Mawlānā Isḥāq Sandhelwī and Mawlānā Asbāṭ Nadwī. When Mawlānā Asbāṭ became blind near the end of his life, he rendered assistance to him in the preparations of his lectures and read to him from various books that he needed. He surpassed all his peers in every stage of his studies, and his teachers well-recognized and respected his efforts and achievements.

He was assigned a teaching post at Nadwah in 1379/1959, which he fulfilled in an exemplary way. He was made the dean of the College of Ḥadīth. There, he taught Ṣaḥīḥ Bukhārī for a total of nineteen years and served as muftī and judge, training students in the same. He was known for his precision in issuing rulings and following the balanced, moderate path of

Nadwah, which was far removed from partisanship and focused on making things easy on people in subsidiary matters. He avoided adding to any conflict or turmoil, and was far above the rigidity of the narrow-minded.

I read to him *'Ilm Uṣūl al-Fiqh* of the eminent scholar and jurist Shaykh 'Abd al-Wahhāb Khalāf, Shāh Walīullah's *al-Fawz al-Ka'bīr*, and parts of al-Marghinānī's *Hidāyat al-Fiqh*. I also learned from him aspects of the Islamic personality as well as many other valuable things. He honored us with his presence at the Imām Bukhārī Conference in Samarqand of 1414/1993 among distinguished scholars of ḥadīth and fiqh headed by our Shaykh Abū al-Ḥasan 'Alī Nadwī and Shaykh 'Abd al-Fattāḥ Abū Ghuddah.

He died on the fifteenth of Jamādī al-Ūlā on 1428/2007 at the age of seventy-three and was buried in the Daliganj cemetery in Lucknow.

His only preoccupation was teaching and busying himself with the matter of issuing rulings and verdicts. He was averse to attending conferences and seminars, as he was the most diligent of people in preserving his time and fulfilling his responsibilities, not tolerating any lapse therein. He was honored with performing Ḥajj in 1410/1990. He was known for his excellent character, patience, piety and refraining from any frivolous pursuits. He was content and righteous, and never seen backbiting anyone or exhibiting ill-will towards others. When someone exhibited animosity towards him, he remained patient and steadfast.

They said: Tell us something about his dialectics. I replied: He allowed students to express their thoughts in a cordial and friendly environment and encouraged them to freely ask questions. Whenever a student sought to understand a case of jurisprudence, he would elaborate on its details, repudiate incorrect positions, and remove any doubts and misgivings. He would involve students in the discussions, such that the entire class would quickly turn into a debate. Students of Nadwah were affiliated with a wide range of juristic and theological schools of thought, and the shaykh would never express preference for any one of these views except in heated debates and arguments within the classroom when his views were openly challenged. He lived his entire life exemplifying good treatment of his students, being cheerful in front of them, and patient towards their often ill conduct. He never exhibited animosity or hatred towards anyone and loved all his students, irrespective of personal affiliations. In turn, they greatly respected him for his knowledge, understanding and good virtues.

They asked: Did he ever get angry? I replied: Never, despite the proliferation of reasons and causes for anger. Once, some students from south India who were Shāfiʿī and Ahl al-Ḥadīth in juristic affiliation and did not know the Urdu language well, addressed him with words that were considered offensive to elders and adults. He neither repudiated them nor did he express any measure of annoyance, or even point out their folly and ill conduct. We never saw him being vengeful or hateful, but he was always cheerful and jolly.

Harms and Benefits of Dialectics

They asked: What is the benefit of dialectics? I replied: It represents critical thinking on differences of intellectual as well as practical nature, and investigating their evidences in order to uncover the truth.

They asked: And what are its harms? I replied: It is harmful if it involves any form of ill-intentions, covering up the truth, exhibiting falsehood, belittling or ridiculing the opponent, blind animosity, or worldly goals such as seeking fame, money or position.

They asked: Do you advise us to learn and become proficient in it? I replied: There is no harm in you practicing it during your learning and education in order to realize its pure aims, but be wary of engaging in argumentation and debate in public settings or in front of others, for they stir up doubts and misgivings in the minds of people, and engender animosity, hatred, pride and arrogance. Ibn Mājah narrates that the Prophet said: "Whoever seeks knowledge in order to argue with the foolish, to show off before scholars, or to attract people's attention, God will admit him to Hell."[136] Ibn Mājah, Ibn Hibbān, and Bayhaqī also relate from Jābir that the Prophet, peace be upon him, said, "Do not seek knowledge in order to show off in front of scholars, or to argue with the foolish, and do not choose the best seat in a gathering for this, for whoever does that, the Fire, the Fire (awaits him)."[137]

---

[136] Sunan Ibn Mājah: al-Muqaddimah.

[137] Ibid.

25

WISDOM, GOOD INSTRUCTION AND ARGUMENT

They asked: What is the meaning of the verse: "Invite to the way of your Lord with wisdom and good instruction, and argue with them in a way that is best."?[138] I replied: You would have achieved real success were you to truly understand the meaning of this verse, for most people have neither understood it properly nor applied it correctly.

Know that inviting to our Lord's way (daʿwah) is only realized with two fundamental characteristics: wisdom (all of which is praiseworthy and not restricted by any other thing) and instruction (which is qualified with being 'good' since it can also be inclusive of other types). Furthermore, argument must generally be avoided, even as it is sometimes unavoidable, in which case it is allowed only 'in a way that is best.'

They asked: Why would you say that argument must generally be avoided? I replied: Because God mentioned two matters in a single arrangement (wisdom and good instruction), as two basic ways of calling to God, and these do not include argumentation. Rather, argument has a different benefit, and for this reason, when it is mentioned, it is separated from the first two matters.

They said: Tell us then the meaning of wisdom. I replied: It includes everything that is firmly established, and here it refers to all matters built upon the 'the natural disposition which God has instilled into man'[139] and supported by sound reasoning. Anything based in the natural disposition of man and supported by sound reasoning is solid and firm. It is incumbent upon believers to call others to God's way by appealing to the most fundamental natural and rational matters. This is summarized by reminding people of God's favors and bounties, as well as His signs and attributes. All of these are natural and rational. These include the notions of associating partners with

---

[138] Qur'ān 16:125.
[139] Qur'ān 30:30.

the Lord (shirk), worshipping Him, and obeying Him. It includes the necessity of rejecting ingratitude to God and shirk,[140] and the ideas of treating others well, especially one's parents. For this very reason, the Qur'ān begins with praise for God, Lord of the worlds, since praise is the beginning and most important part of one's innate natural disposition.

Many people who call to God today have distorted the process because they have not understood the meaning of wisdom. Thus, they build their efforts upon proving the existence of God, and affirming his Lordship and sustenance through rational proofs. This is a serious mistake. God has placed within the roots of our nature the need to love Him and be grateful to Him, and this is further supported by our rational intellects. What these people attempt to affirm through their rational arguments can easily be reversed, thereby losing any benefits to their proclamations. This was not the way of the Prophets and Messengers at all. In fact, Satan affirmed the Lordship of God despite being the greatest unbeliever. This is also the origin of the mistake of theologians and mystics in their misguided explanations of the meanings of God's oneness (tawḥīd).

On the other hand, relying on basic natural and reasonable matters are the firmest proofs and most solid evidences. When a person adopts wisdom in his affairs, it makes the best impression on others. For instance, if a thirsty person came across an old woman sitting by a well and said, "Dear mother, I am thirsty. Would you please allow me to drink some water?" She would likely be pleased by his good manners and allow him to drink from the sweet water, and even give him something to eat. However, were the same person to come to her and say, "Wife of my father, give me water!"; she would likely raise her cane to hit him! Respect for elders and addressing them in a manner that suits their rank is embedded in one's nature and supported by reason. The same goes for the notion of admiration for those who are polite and kind in their requests.

They asked: Tell us the meaning of good instruction. I replied: It is reminding people of the days of God (i.e. the stories of past nations, whom God has rewarded or punished in anyway), and of death and the Day of Judgment in all its details. It should be noted that this can potentially lead to rejection if the warning becomes excessive to the point of making people despair and become hopeless before their Lord. That is bad instruction and

[140] Associating partners with God.

should be avoided. God's Book is filled with reminders of the days of God, of death, resurrection, paradise and Hellfire.

They said: Tell us about arguing in the best way. I replied: You must first know, as I already mentioned, that argumentation is not one of the ways of calling to God at all. However, if such a situation happens to arise for a person calling to God, then he must first realize that this represents a distraction from his efforts. This person should think critically and decide: either they disregard the distraction altogether, or point out the weakness of the opponent's evidences and refute them, before promptly returning to the da'wah.

An example in the Qur'ān of disregarding argumentation meant to distract is as follows:

> Pharaoh said: "And who is this Lord of the Universe?" Mūsā answered: "The Lord of the heavens and the earth and of all that is between them, if you were only to believe." Pharaoh said to those around him: "Do you hear (what he says)?" Moses said: "(He is) Your Lord and the Lord of your first forefathers." Pharaoh said to the audience: "This Messenger of yours who has been sent to you is simply mad." Mūsā continued: "(He is) the Lord of the east and the west, and all between them. If you only had any understanding!"[141]

An example of pointing out the weakness of an argument and refuting it is as follows:

> Have you not considered the case of the person who had an argument with Ibrāhīm simply because God had given him kingship. When Ibrāhīm said, "My Lord is He Who gives life and causes death," he answered, "I give life and cause death." Then Ibrāhīm said, "Then, God brings the sun from the east: just bring it from the west." At this, the disbeliever was confounded. And God does not guide those who are unjust.[142]

---

[141] Qur'ān 26:23-28.

[142] Qur'ān 2:258.

They asked: What is the benefit of argumentation then? I replied: Basically there are some people who are so endowed with the luxuries of worldly life that they are deluded by their own arguments and are not aware of the weakness and frailty that they contain. So, when someone wise and rational is able to come and show the fragility of their claims, the person becomes perplexed and confounded, weakening his stance among his associates and making him utterly incapable of opposing the caller.

26

WHO TAUGHT YOU TO WRITE

They asked: We are amazed by your fine and prolific Arabic, chock full of interesting and elegant expressions which are, at the same time wonderful and clear. Were you raised in the deserts of the Najd province,[143] weeping over its ruins and remains? Or did you spend your youth in the plains of Tihāmah,[144] vacillating between its rugged terrain and mountainous landscape? I replied: Neither did I grow up in the Najd desert, being nourished by its milk, nor did the Quraysh give me noble shelter in its quarters. Rather, I am a foreigner with respect to Arabic and reached my prime in the countryside of India. I am neither fated for greatness, nor do I possess the least amount of glory. I am simply one of the many students of this language who happen to love it dearly and am devoted to it.

They asked: How can you write so well in it when you are not native to it? I replied: Just as so many thousands from the past and present excelled in it.

They said: We are non-native like you and so many others, who achieved proficiency, took the lead and went really far. We would like to emulate them and aim for the same. We would like to follow their way and manner, and tread their path. Can you tell us, based on your insight, who was the one who trained and cultured you in writing? I replied: I learned writing from many teachers in my native Jawnpūr and at Nadwah.

How Maulānā Wāḍiḥ Taught Us Composition

They asked: Which of them had the greatest influence on you in developing this wonderful and valuable ability? I replied: He was our teacher Mawlānā Muḥammad Wāḍiḥ Rashīd Nadwī, scion of pure Arab heritage, finest specimen of Muḍar,[145] heir to the glory of ʿAdnān.[146]

---

[143] The ancient highlands of central Arabia.

[144] Coastal region in western Arabia.

[145] One of the prominent ancestors of the Arabs, to the point that Ibn Khaldūn even referred to Arabic as the language of Muḍar.

[146] Descendent of Ismāʿīl and forefather of the Arabs.

They said: Describe for us in a sufficient way his way of teaching the skill of writing, so that we may become closer to our goals. I replied: I will elaborate on that in four points:

Firstly, he would point us to the best contemporary writers and endear us to read their books and articles in order to strengthen our readings skills, increase our linguistic yield, examine various kinds of writing, and comprehend multiple forms and types of expression. We would also be taught to reflect on the points of beauty in thought, emotion and style among the masters of Arabic literature and expression. We would learn from them in order to further our own explorations of the meanings of life. We would become familiar with the culture, civilization and trends of the Arab world. We would learn the pressing issues of our ummah and our times. We would understand our own position with respect to our heritage in terms of ethics, etiquette, customs and inclinations.

Secondly, he would develop in us the proficiency to translate Arabic to Urdu, and from Arabic to English and Urdu. This would increase our understanding of our own mother language and make us more grounded in Arabic terminology and construction. It would increase our cultural inventory and help us comprehend more precisely what we read and write. We would try our best to understand the text we were translating, extract equivalent and alternative words in Arabic, and then convey the ideas and meanings of the text in a way that would make our writing natural and not simply forced or artificial.

Thirdly, he trained us in creative writing by making us author articles, comment on news, and critique literary techniques, political ideas, or religious and social views. He would stimulate our own natural skills and abilities and motivate us to think and draw conclusions. He inspired us to be persistent in expressing ourselves and reporting our views, as a way to train us to explore our own thoughts, opinions, feelings and needs, and then to express them in a logical and orderly manner in sound Arabic. He would raise our level of thinking to become creative and innovative, using our words to achieve feeling and sentiment, and evoke imagination.

Fourthly, he would encourage us to publish our articles in the journal *al-Rā'id* which he used to preside over. This would develop our confidence in ourselves and in our literary and linguistic abilities. He would select texts, news reports, and comments, for us to translate. Sometimes we would develop new ideas extracted from our own life experiences or from our readings, and then put them down in writing. We would review these and develop them further in more precise and eloquent ways, and then present them to him for publication. He would then correct these to make them ready for the level of a newspaper.

They asked: Who were some of the contemporary writers whose books your teacher recommended reading? I replied: The most eminent of them was Aḥmad Amīn, Tāhā Ḥusayn, Muṣṭafā Sibā'ī, Muṣṭafā Luṭfī al-Manfalūṭī, Sayyid Qutb, 'Alī al-Ṭanṭāwī and Muṣṭafā Amīn.

They asked: Did he not warn you of some of their views, especially Tāhā Ḥusayn? I replied: Of course. He would always direct us to what was sound Islamic thought, with fatherly care and concern, and without taking away our freedom to read and think for ourselves. He would counter some of the distorted views of Tāhā Ḥusayn by referring us to the writings of Shaykh Abū al-Ḥasan 'Alī Nadwī and others of sound and balanced Islamic thinking.

They asked: How did he correct and remediate your linguistic mistakes? I replied: This question is dangerously pleasing. I have never seen a person perfect the art of correcting others like he did, for he was amazing in that. With his corrections, he would strive to preserve our original ideas as much as possible.

They asked: Did he ever get angry with any of your mistakes? I replied: I never saw him express irritation or annoyance with any mistake, however great it was. Rather, he was open to all mistakes, diligent on correcting them, open-hearted and welcoming. We loved him from the bottom of our hearts and the depths of our souls.

They said: Perhaps it was because you had so few mistakes on your part. I replied: No, but our mistakes were many and some even ridiculous and shameful. But he had a magnanimous character, noble temperament, pure thought process, and an ever-cheerful attitude. He would cover up other people's mistakes and overlook their faults and errors. He would never confront us with anything that would hurt us. Every day the curtains of the night would lift to reveal a new noble trait he possessed.

They said: If only all teachers were like that. I replied: Educational institutes are barren from producing the likes of him. Let his age be long so knowledge can enjoy his beautiful craft and his continuous beneficence!

They said: We don't know if we are more amazed by your teacher's educational manner or his elevated and noble treatment of his students. I replied: All of his students and colleagues share your sentiment. His heavenly and elevated character was no less than his raised status in education and training. God bless his life and deeds.

❁27❁

HOW SHOULD YOU WRITE AN ARTICLE?

They asked: How should you write an article? I replied: The answer essentially consists of two parts. First, what can be considered to be a well-written article? That involves the following:

1. The topic of the essay should be defined completely and precisely in your mind with full clarity.
2. The intended aim of this topic should also be clear in your mind.
3. The organization and order of the different components of the essay should be conceptually clear in your mind with no ambiguity regarding the reasons behind this arrangement.
4. The structuring of the article and its division into sections and chapters should be done on a rational basis and in a scholarly fashion so that the discussions and arguments in the article move in an organized and logical order from one point to another.
5. Commit yourself with full scholarly responsibility to use the fewest amount of words possible and the minimum use of technical terminology in order to prove any point of discussion, and if the anticipated reader is not accustomed to any of this terminology, then be sure to explain them whenever they are used.
6. Similarly, with complete scholarly responsibility, avoid using the kind of language which is aimed to keep the meaning and interpretation of the topic obscure or vague, or which under the guise of its mesmerizing language or claims masks the author's true intentions and objectives. The correct approach is that a good essay attempts to provide clear information and not to impress or mesmerize anyone.
7. At the end of the article, reiterate the main points and the major steps in reasoning behind the research conclusions, and do not needlessly write a divergent ending or conclusion to the essay.

Secondly, how does one prepare himself to write an article? The answer to that is:

1. First, the reason for writing the article should be clear in your mind. This does not just mean that the topic should be clear, for that has already been established. But it means that the intended purpose of writing on the topic should be clear to you. For example, the purpose could be that it is your homework, or that there is considerable misunderstanding regarding the topic in the minds of people and you would like to remove those misgivings.
2. You should aim to know, as much as possible, who is going to be reading the article and for what purpose. For example, a teacher reading your article intended as homework would aim to see how much of his teaching you have understood, or your colleagues would read your article with the intention of either competing or cooperating with you.
3. The limits and purview of the article should be absolutely clear in your mind. This means that before starting the article you should clearly know what the most important and relevant issues are to your research. For example, what are the various authors' works that are required reading for your essay, and what are the issues and points that will appear prominently in the course of your discussion? If you're intent on writing the essay, you will put special emphasis on the scope and purview of the article.
4. Choose the most appropriate way to prove the various portions of your article. Some parts of the article may require proven statistical data analysis, while others may require experiential proofs, and yet others the reference of past scholars. So where there exists a requirement for validation by past scholars, if you were to use your personal experiences as proofs—or the opposite—then this would make the article weak and less academic.
5. The process and arguments for proving your research conclusions should be clear in your mind as much as possible.

You should ask yourself whether all these steps are mutually connected and reinforce one other. This means that you should prove each single claim, one after the other, and establish a logical connection between them.

6. You should be very clear about the scope and implications of the article, the attitudes and expectations of your expected readers, and the introductions and assumptions behind them as much as possible.
7. If you are satisfied with all the above action points, and you believe that the purpose of your article is really to provide knowledge to yourself or to others, and not simply to impress, amaze or mesmerize anyone, then keep in mind the priorities and organization of the points of analysis you wish to present, and start writing the article.

28

LUCKNOW[147]

From an early age, I had been quite fond of attending sermons and lessons, to come and go as I please, and to acquire from them what softens the heart and refines the soul. When I first began my journey and took my due portion of knowledge and manners, I resolved to travel and journey afar in its path. I forced myself to renounce my companions. I began to set out for the land of Arnū but my heart settled on Lucknow. Though, I hailed from Jawnpūr, abode of splendor and joy, I remained patient with its separation.

I bid farewell to my parents and kin, who were upset about my leaving. I could not bear the decision, as a young man whose home was now gone. The train began to move, passing flat and desolate wastelands. I had embarked on danger, in order to reap the fruits. I arrived at the capital of the state, home to splendid buildings and structures, land of culture and education. I found it as tongues had described it. It contained all that souls could crave for and eyes could feast upon.

I joined Nadwat al-'Ulamā' and felt as if I had been raised from the dusty ground to the stars up above, from the level earth to the high heavens. I came across ancient books and studied with great teachers who were knowledgeable scholars, learned scribes and pious worshippers, all of noble origins and stock. They were scholars of reports and transmissions, and men of keen understanding. They were blessed with great manners, while the sciences lay at their feet. They adorned every place and brought honor to every time. They were builders of monuments of glory, and persons of great merit and virtue. They were warriors of the pen and masters of their craft.

---

[147] The *maqāmāt* (singular, *maqām*) is an Arabic literary genre consisting of short poetic passages in a sophisticated rhyme. First invented by al-Hamadhānī (d. 1008) and consummated by al-Ḥarīrī (d. 1122), it has inspired countless writers to compile their thoughts and expressions utilizing it. This chapter on Lucknow, originally titled *al-maqāmah al-lucknawīyyah*, was composed by Dr. Akram Nadwī in this genre. For obvious reasons, it is impossible to replicate the rhyme, metaphors, proverbs and discourse of this genre into any other language. Thus, I have followed in the footsteps of those who translated the gist of the message of these maqāmāt into English without preserving their rhyme, as was done by Thomas Chenery (d. 1884) who translated the first twenty-six sections of *al-Maqāmāt al-Ḥarīrī* in 1867 for the Oriental Translation Fund, with the rest completed by Dr. F. Steingass in 1898.

Nourished on the milk of eloquence, they might have drawn the trail of oblivion over the most powerful orator. I was delighted by what they provided and rejoiced at their instruction. Their company nourished me and removed my sorrow.

I experienced there the luxury of true friendship and brotherhood, discovering sincere friends and truthful companions. Great and powerful bonds developed between us. They were suns and stars of learning, known for dignity, humility, intelligence, faithfulness, loyalty, excellence and generosity. They were exceedingly generous, even as the era of generosity had long passed and left the affairs in the hands of the wicked. You would find them grateful for God's favors and patient with God's decree. They were lenient and flexible, and made things easy. They were bearers of excellent virtues, pure of heart, tender and loving, and far from malice and ill-will. Their dreams weighed down upon mountains, and their personalities rejected conflict. They shunned the ignorant and foolish ones and were far away from the arrogant and haughty. They remained so until time separated them from their bodies, flinging them to vast distances and lands. Yet their hearts remained intertwined and unseparated, like the flow of water. These are my brothers, God bless them in every state, virtuous of speech and tongue, noble of conduct and action.

I will single out for mention ʿAbd al-Ḥayy. If you met him, it were as if you had laid your eyes upon Ḥātim al-Ṭāʾī,[148] a young man whom God had blessed with upright conduct, extreme generosity, and praiseworthy temperament. His conduct was more radiant than the brightest flowers, and his merits shone brighter than light. His words were more delicate than the morning breeze. He had pure and refined characteristics which rose to levels none of his peers could reach. He drank fully from the cup of generosity and openhandedness, and loved everyone far and near. He befriended people and spent money on them, never changing this habit to the end. He was a servant to all guests who visited him, profusely granting them provisions whether they were coming or going. He was truthful in speech and free of any blame. He did not harbor ill thoughts for anyone, never withheld good and never rebuked. He was a friend to all, and overlooked and found excuses for others' mistakes. He refrained from insulting the wicked ones, but treated them honorably instead. He was forbearing as much as possible, and no dirt

[148] Famous pre-Islamic poet known for his generosity, and father of the Companion ʿAdīyy b. Ḥātim.

could soil his virtues. Women are barren of giving birth to the likes of him. I received from him true love and returned it in kind. How can I forget him when his remembrance is ever abiding? How can I deny even one of his merits?

All his gatherings were the finest, and his words were like pearls. Whenever I spent time in his company, I found him surrounded by people. Once he wanted to advise those of us who were close to him. He awakened us from slumber and warned us of its consequences. He invited us to a banquet and brought all types of food and drink, sweet to the palate and difficult to describe with words. The audience fell upon the food, attacking it without refinement or gentleness. Then he charmed us with conversation, and we spent the evening with these scattered pearls. He addressed us with speech, and we enjoyed portions of songs. We narrated chains of ḥadīth and enjoyed listening to them. A type of intoxication came over us, and sleep began to depart from our eyes. The presence of loved ones and the magnet of company is nourishment for the soul.

When we finished eating and stopped our conversations, ʿAbd al-Ḥayy stood up to address us, and the position was very strange. He said: The one I will never disparage narrates to me:

My father left me when I was young. I was raised as an indigent orphan. My mother cared for me and gave flight to my worries. We were afflicted by hunger, misery, destitution and poverty. We were exhausted and worn out. Even strangers and opponents grieved over us. When I got older and witnessed both good and bad days, I began to fully experience and explore life. I adopted trade as a means to acquire wealth and profit, until I became independent. I began to enjoy life and comfort, and I became wealthy and rich. But my neck bore the necklace of perfidy, and I had a contemptuous manner and arrogant swagger. I loved to brag endlessly, boast among the elite and oppress the poor, weak and orphaned ones. Worldly life is surely a plague for most people, most of whom transgress whenever they are affluent.

One day, in one of my travels I came across the abode of the deceased, a place of bones and remains. I saw some people digging a grave, while others wept and still others counseled patience. When we finished the burial and grief was heavy upon all, they asked one of their shaykhs to give them a reminder and admonition. The people gathered around him.

He said: 'For the like of this, then, let them labor, those who labor [in God's way]!'[149] Hold your tears and your eyes, those who cry and weep! Prepare yourselves, negligent ones! Take heed, those who are insightful! Every person shall taste death, every soul extinguished, and every voice silenced. Life is only a limited number of breaths. You are in a short-lived abode, whose end is near. Be aware of the end of this life, and leave all desires for what is to be feared. Be sorrowful over the burial of your companions and frightful of the true nature of the dirt. Perhaps the same grave shall become a grave for others, laughing at the congested conglomeration of these opposite personas. How many are buried over the remains of other buried ones, over the long passage of time? These graves conceal many strong hands, and the tombs include the best and most noble families. Remember 'when all the contents of the graves will be poured forth, and all that is in the hearts will be laid bare.'[150]

Human beings, wake up from your sleep, and rise from your stupor! You do not engage in the permissible, nor abstain from the forbidden. You do not content yourselves with limits in this worldly life, nor do you avoid greed and evil. You do not heed reminders and exhortations, nor are you changed by warning. You chase desires and strike in the dark, progressing in ignorance and infatuated by deviation. You are obstinately extravagant and carelessly blind. You readily adopt doubts and plunge into temptation. You are easily caught up in intrigues and are enthusiastic for ruin. Do you think that you will be left in vain, and not be held to account tomorrow? You built your home here but what have you done for your other home? Every person one day will ride his own vessel, over the necks of his enemies and relatives. The tombs are desirous of you, however much you hate that, and they keep increasing. They are being supplied every single day, and no one ever comes back from them. I see the earth continuing to remain while its dwellers keep perishing. Glad tidings to those who listen and take heed: those who forbid their souls from vain desires, are certain that their salvation lies in paying attention, and that people 'only get what they strive for, that their striving shall soon be seen, and that they shall then be fully recompensed.'[151]

This exhortation touched the hearts and softened their hardness. We found ourselves unable to describe it. He had surpassed Ibn al-Jawzī and Ibn

[149] Qur'ān 37:61.
[150] Qur'ān 100:9-10.
[151] Qur'ān 53:39-41.

Sam'ūn and made the tears of all flow profusely. Everyone rushed to repentance, stretching their hands out in supplication and prayer and turning their heads up to the heavens.

The narrator said: I returned to my home with a fearful heart and altered color. I was afraid and fearful of wronging others and all other evils. I was ever-aware of the matters of death and the grave, and ever-reminded of the day when all shall stand before the Lord of the worlds.

When 'Abd al-Ḥayy was done, all of us were fully aware of our end. Our eyelids were moist with tears, and our anxiety was overpowering. Looking within, we found ourselves lacking. We became repentant and penitent before our Lord, humble and ready to turn to Him again and again.

29

OH STRANGER AMONG HIS PEERS AND TIME!

Remembering Maulānā Wāḍiḥ Rashīd Nadwī

'Alī b. al-Madīnī said: "A person cannot be measured except by his own peers and by his own times. I once stated that Sa'īd was more knowledgeable than Ḥammād b. Zayd (d. 179/795). That reached Yaḥyā b. Sa'īd al-Qaṭṭān and he found it difficult to consider that a person could be compared to those who were in an earlier generation, such that someone would say, for instance, that Sufyān (d. 161/778) is more knowledgeable than Sha'bī (d. 103/723), or ask what Sha'bī possessed that Sufyān did not." It was said to 'Alī that someone had claimed that Mālik (d. 179/795) was more learned than Zuhrī (d. 124/741). He replied: "I do not compare Mālik with Zuhrī, nor do I compare Zuhrī with Sa'īd b. al-Musayyab (d. 94/715). All people are in their own time."

Let those who agree with Yaḥyā and 'Alī agree with them, and let those who differ, differ. As for me, I agree with them entirely and am utterly impressed by their opinion. I consider their statements to reflect their deep grasp and keen understanding. And who can ever match Yaḥyā and 'Alī? I have seen our teacher and brother, the pious scholar Aḥmad 'Āshūr of Madīnah comment on this principle and make an exclusion when he said: "This represents true justice for the contemporary writer that he be compared only according to his own era and contemporaries, even as he is far less in stature than those that came before him, while it may still be possible that the later ones can surpass the earlier ones."

But, there is no general rule without their existing an exception to it. I find myself today as keen as I can be to follow the way of Aḥmad 'Āshūr, but there seems to be a strong impulse within me to exclude from that rule our teacher Muḥammad Wāḍiḥ Rashīd Nadwī, with all due respect to Yaḥyā and 'Alī—as much as I hate to detract from their statements.

Oh Abū Ja'far! How can we compare you to your peers or to your era? Do you resemble them in any way, and they to you? You were a stranger to them, and they to you! They opposed your method and departed from your way. But are time and place the only peers? Are not the peers of a person those who share his characteristics and resemble his character? Are not the humble ones brothers, the abstinent ones close associates, and the same for those who are pious and fearful? Are they not real peers, even as their times and eras may diverge and their locations be far apart?

Oh Shaykh of ours, who was a stranger among his own peers and contemporaries! You were a peer to the past instead, pushed away by time and place. You excelled with your special character, manners, and excellent traits. Our Lord gave you to us out of His favor and grace. In turn, we were well-pleased with your shining merits. Your beauty filled the eyes of beholders, and your merits praised by those near and far.

We narrate from Layth that when more than three people sat with Abū al-ʿĀliyah, he would get up. Abū Bakr b. ʿAyyāsh asked Aʿmash, "What was the highest number of people you saw with Ibrāhīm al-Nakhaʿī?" He replied, "Four or five." Ibrāhīm b. Bashshār states that he heard Ibrāhīm b. Adham say, "Whoever seeks knowledge for God, then obscurity is far more beloved to that person than fame."

Did you not resemble Abū al-ʿĀliyah and Ibrāhīm in hating that people crowd around you? Did you not far prefer obscurity to fame? Did you not abandon the world for those who fought over it and competed for wealth and inevitable ruin?

ʿAbdullah b. Marzūq once asked Sufyān al-Thawrī for advice on where to settle down. He replied, "By the Mountain of Ẓahrān[152] so that no one would recognize you." Sufyān used to say, "I see that the best thing for a person is to enter into a hole, in order to distance themselves from temptation." He also used to say, "Had I not feared humiliation, I would have lived among a people that did not recognize me." ʿAbd al-Raḥmān b. Mahdī narrates from Ṭālūt: I heard Ibrāhīm b. Adham say, "A servant who loves fame is not sincere to God." ʿAbd al-Qādir Jīlānī said, "I wish I was once again in the desert and wilderness as I used to be in the past, not seeing people and without them seeing me."

Was not seclusion from people one of your traits? How close you were to Sufyān in tending to your own affairs and avoiding all that didn't concern you! Every single person that knew you testified that you did not like fame

---

[152] Eastern coastal Arabia.

nor anything that led to it. Your words continued to echo and sound the truth while you clung to the confines of your home.

Yaḥyā b. Abī Kathīr said, "The pillars of humility are three: being satisfied with lower ranks in assemblies; initiating the greetings upon meeting someone; and hating praise, fame or the showcasing of one's good deeds." Ṣāliḥ al-Murrī relates that once Ḥasan, Yūnus and Ayyūb were discussing the notion of humility when Ḥasan said, "Humility is to leave your house and consider every single Muslim you meet to be better than you."

In this vein, you shunned position and rank in all forums and councils, preferring to humbly sit in the audience with students and others. You never claimed to have knowledge or virtue over anyone, nor claimed any honor or rank for yourself. You despised commendation and praise, and turned away from those who sought to flatter you or praise you. You put yourself in the lowest rank possible and always preferred others to yourself.

Sufyān al-Thawrī said, "The most beneficial clothes are those that are easiest upon you." Whoever saw your clothes would presume that they were worth very little. But within those very clothes they would have encountered a soul that had achieved the heights of honor, and come across a radiant star within grasp without ever having traversed the distance. You were so far from your partners in terms of glory and dominion. You were but a bright moon by whose light seekers and travelers were guided.

Abū al-Dardā' said, "Learn silence just as you learn speech, for silence represents a great part of forbearance. Be far more eager to listen than to speak, and never speak about that which does not concern you. Never laugh without purpose, nor walk without purpose." Ibrāhīm al-Nakhai said, "They would sit and review, and the most silent ones were considered the best of them." 'Abdullah b. al-Sindī relates that a man came to Sufyān al-Thawrī and greeted him in an extended form, saying: 'Peace be on you, Oh Abū 'Abdullah, and His mercy and blessings. How are you and how are things?' Sufyān replied, "God forgive us and you! We are not those who prolong things."

Silence, dear shaykh, was an expression of your manner and derived from your character. People engage in speech with the purpose of being concise, but most of the time, silence would have been far better. Whoever is incapable of good silence is even more incapable of conveying his words effectively. You were so far removed from being excessive and avoided elaboration. It was as if you weighed each word prior to uttering it and protected yourself from frivolity and exaggeration.

Aḥmad b. Ibrāhīm b. Bashshār relates that he asked Ibrāhīm b. Adham about worship, and he replied, "The pillar of worship is deliberation and silence, except for the remembrance of God." Similarly, you were always reflecting and brought to us deep knowledge and precise understanding. You observed prolonged silence and when you spoke, it was always with wisdom and brevity. Ismā'īl b. Umayyah relates that 'Aṭā' also observed prolonged silence, and when he spoke it appears to us that he was being helped." Likewise, you were very wise and mature. How different are wisdom and foolishness, or guidance and misguidance!

It was narrated that Abū Ḥanīfah, Bukhārī and other early figures never engaged in speaking ill of others. Some wise men have related that when a person spoke ill of another in the presence of scholars, they would say to that person: "You have proven your own faults by exposing the faults of others, for the one who seeks out others' faults does so in accordance with that which he himself possesses." Ibn al-Kawwā' said to Rabī' b. Khaytham, "We have never seen you speak ill of another nor blame him." He replied, "Woe to you Ibn al-Kawwā'! I am not so pleased with myself that I forget my own faults in order to speak about others! People too often fear God over the faults of others while feeling safe about their own." 'Abd al-Raḥmān b. 'Umar relates that he heard 'Abd al-Raḥmān b. Mahdī say, "Had it not been that I hate to see God disobeyed, I would have loved that every single person in this land expose me and backbite me. What is more delightful than a person finding good deeds in his scale on the Day of Judgment that he had done which he did not know about."

Can this description be truthfully applied to other than you? You lived your life while people were safe from your tongue and hands. You were an adequate partner to them, never blaming, censuring or rebuking anyone.

'Abd al-Raḥmān b. Mahdī said, "Let a person fear bad character just as he fears the forbidden." Fuḍayl b. 'Iyāḍ said, "We did not distinguish people by the abundance of their prayers or fasts, but due to their generous souls, sound hearts and sincerity for others."

Similarly, you were this way in your own esteemed character and sincerity towards your companions and students. You had sweet conduct and a welcoming heart. You treated people as companions, were patient with misfortune, and bore every offense from adversaries and well-wishers.

Those after you could not find your likes except in your own brother, for you two were true kin in character and manners, both possessing nobility and rank, twin branches of the same tree, plants from the same seed, and without parallel.

We were amazed to see in you a picture of the pious predecessors, ancestry that raised you to the confines of honor and glory, described with piety, abstinence, and acts of worship that lead to eternal gardens. We are sorry that people compare us with you expecting that we follow your life and example. How can those who are handicapped and broken even begin to comprehend the stature of those who are skilled and knowledgeable? How can one who is artificial and contrived imitate one who was original and unique? It is hideous injustice that there are those who seek to find for you peers or companions in your own time and land!

I for one shall surely never forget you, noble Shaykh of ours! How can I forget the one who reminds me that there was no-one of his caliber or like? Let me be blamed, for when I remember you, emotions gush forth with love and passion, one after the other, without stopping or tiring. Let the enemies know that I am here in the land of the West, full of sorrow and gloom over you.

God have mercy on you, Abū Jaʿfar! May He reward you with that which is most precious with Him, and admit you into the gardens of bliss!

30

WHAT ARE YOU?

They said: You have authored *al-Fiqh al-Islāmī*[153] on the jurisprudential rules according to the school of Abū Ḥanīfah and collected all of the school's evidences therein. You have also written a biography on him, so you must be a Ḥanafī.

Then they said: But then we have seen you combining prayers while travelling[154] and allowing wiping over cloth socks.[155] You do not mind if your students follow a particular Imām in jurisprudence or even if they follow no-one at all. So you must be a *ghayr muqallid*.[156]

They said: You must be Ash'arī[157] since you graduated from Nadwat al-'Ulamā' and all the religious schools in India are Ash'arī. But then we have seen you speak highly of Maulānā Shiblī Nu'mānī and go to great lengths in praising, honoring and revering him, while he was a Māturīdī,[158] so you must be Māturīdī. Then we saw you teach *al-'Aqīdah al-Ṭaḥāwīyah*[159] and you refuted both the Ash'arīs and Māturīdī while preferring the school of the salaf (early predecessors), so then you must be a Salafī.

They said: You pray in the Central Mosque of Oxford which is an institution of the Barelwī group,[160] so you must be Barelwī. But we have seen you sit with the scholars of Deoband and their elders, so you must be

---

153 Nadwī, Moḥammad Akram. *Al-Fiqh al-Islāmī.* London, UK: Angelwing Media. 2012.

154 In the Ḥanafī school, the predominant opinion does not allow the combining of prayers in a state of travel, while all the other schools allow it.

155 The validity of wiping over normal, cloth socks in lieu of washing the feet for ablution is debated among legal schools. The most vocal voices in the Ḥanafī school do not allow it.

156 This term, literally meaning 'not a blind follower,' is often used in a derogatory sense by strict adherents of the jurisprudential schools to refer to those that do not adhere to them at all.

157 Theological school attributed to its founder Abū al-Ḥasan 'Alī al-Ash'arī (d. 324/936).

158 Theological school attributed to Abū Manṣūr Māturīdī of Samarqand (d. 333/944) that closely resembles the Ash'arī school.

159 One of the earliest texts authored on the subject of creed by the Ḥanafī traditionist of Egypt Abū Ja'far al-Ṭaḥāwī (d. 321/933).

160 A religious group in the Indian subcontinent founded by Aḥmad Riḍā Khān (d. 1340/1921) that fiercely upholds certain Sufi practices and beliefs.

Deobandī then. Then we saw you pray Jumu'ah and intermingle with Arabs, getting along with them while they are Wahhābīs, so you must be Wahhābī.

They said: You go out with Tablīghī Jamā'at group,[161] so you must be Tablīghī. But then we have seen you criticize their narration of rejected and baseless ḥadīths, so you must be from Jamā'at Islāmī,[162] especially since many of your friends belong to this movement, and you frequently visit their centers to teach and give talks. Then we have seen that you love Ḥasan al-Banna the martyr and praise his book *Mudhakkirāt al-da'wah wa al-dā'iyyah*. And you are impressed with the books *al-Taṣwīr al-fannī fī al-Qur'ān* and *Mashāhid yawm al-qiyāmah* written by Sayyid Quṭb and *Du'āt lā quḍāt* written by Ḥasan al-Ḥudaybī, so you must be Ikhwānī.[163]

They said: You read *Iḥyā' 'ulūm al-dīn* of Ghazālī and narrate its stories to people. And you regularly read the *Mathnawī* of Rūmī,[164] use his poetic verses as evidence, and show your love for him, so you must be a Sufi. But we have seen you criticize Ibn 'Arabī[165] and those who support the doctrine of 'waḥdat al-wujūd.'[166] You also criticize the spiritual states and stations of the people of taṣawwuf and absolve yourself of their discourses and ecstatic utterances. So, you are from the followers of Imām Ibn Taymiyyah. We have seen you attach great importance to him and encouraging your colleagues and students to read his books.

They said: Your situation is truly obscure to us. So tell us: What are you? Do you belong to any single one of these groups while deceptively befriending the others? Or are you a *lā madhhabī*?[167] Or are you a diplomatic politician protecting your interests and what will benefit you by linking

---

[161] Religious missionary movement founded in India in 1925 by Mawlānā Muḥammad Ilyās (d. 1302/1885).

[162] Islamic movement founded by the revivalist scholar Mawlānā Mawdūdī (d. 1399/1979).

[163] The Muslim Brotherhood, or *al-Ikhwān al-Muslimūn*, was an Islamic movement founded in Egypt in 1928 by the charismatic scholar Ḥasan al-Banna, who was assassinated in 1368/1949. It went on to become the single most influential group in the Muslim world, and its figures included Ḥasan al-Ḥudaybī (d. 1393/1973) who succeeded al-Banna as its leader, and Sayyid Quṭb (executed by Egyptian authorities in 1386/1966).

[164] Celebrated poet, scholar, mystic and theologian from Khurāsān who died in Konya 672/1273. He is described as the best-selling poet in the United States of America.

[165] Celebrated mystic and theologian from Murcia, Spain who died in 638/1240.

[166] This doctrine that there is no real distinction between the creation and the Creator.

[167] This term, meaning 'belonging to no legal school,' is used as a slur and is synonymous with the previously mentioned term *ghayr muqallid.*

yourself with each of the many parties and disparate groups? Tell us: What are you?

I replied: *I believe in God, His angels, His books, His Messengers, the Day of Judgement, destiny, with its good and evil both coming from God, and resurrection after death.*

They said: We are not asking about that, for we all believe in what you have mentioned. Rather we are asking about your belonging and the name you choose for yourself.

I replied: God has said: *"He named you Muslims."*[168] So I am a Muslim, son of Islam, and brother to Muslims.

They replied: You have only made us more perplexed about you, and we have never been as confused about you as we are today.

---

[168] Qur'ān 22:78.

REFERENCES

Al-Akili, Muhammad. *The Beauty of the Righteous & Ranks of the Elite*. Philadelphia, US: Pearl Publishing House. 1995.

Al-'Asqalānī, Ibn Ḥajar. *Fatḥ al-bārī*. 2nd edition. Egypt: Dār al-'Ālamiyyah. 1436/2015.

Brown, Jonathan A.C. *Hadith: Muhammad's Legacy in the Medieval and Modern World*. London, UK: Oneworld Publications. 2nd edition. 2018.

Dhahabī, Shams al-Dīn Muḥammad b. Aḥmad. *Siyar a'lām al-nubalā'*. Beirut, Lebanon: Mu'assasat al-Risālah. 11th edition. 1417/1996.

Al-Ḥarīrī, al-Qāsim b. 'Alī. *Maqāmāt al-Ḥarīrī*. Beirut, Lebanon: Dār Ṣādir. No date given.

Ḥasanī, 'Abd al-Ḥayy. *Nuzhat al-khawāṭir wa bahjat al-masāmi' wa al-nawāẓir*. Hyderabad, India: Osmania Oriental Publication Bureau. 1382/1962.

Hughes, Thomas Patrick. *Dictionary of Islam*. New Delhi, India: Oriental Books Reprint Corporation. 1976.

Ibn Khaldūn. *The Muqaddimah: An Introduction to History*. Translated by Franz Rosenthal. New Jersey, US: Princeton University Press. 2005.

Ibn Taymiyyah. *Majmū' al-fatāwā*. Madīnah, Saudi Arabia: Majma' al-Mālik Fahd. 1425/2004.

Ibn Taymiyyah. *Majmū' al-fatāwā*. Manṣūrah, Egypt: Dār al-Wafā'. 3rd edition. 1426/2005.

Ibn Taymiyyah. *The Principles of Tafseer*. Birmingham, UK: Al-Hidaayah Publishing & Distribution. 1414/1993.

Ismā'īl, Muḥammad Ḥasan (editor). *Al-siyāsah al-shar'īyah majmū' al-rasā'il*. Beirut, Lebanon: Dār al-Kutub al-'Ilmiyyah. 2003.

Al-Marzūqī, Abū 'Alī Aḥmad b. Muḥammad. *Sharḥ dīwān al-ḥamāsah*. Beirut, Lebanon: Dār al-Kutub al-'Ilmiyyah. 1424/2003.

Montgomery, James. *'Antarah ibn Shaddād: War Songs*. New York, US: New York University Press. 2018.

Nadwī, Abū al-Ḥasan 'Alī. *Al-Imām Muḥammad b. Ismā'īl al-Bukhārī wa Kitābuhū Ṣaḥīḥ al-Bukhārī*. Raebareli, India: Dār 'Arafāt. 1414/1993.

Nadwī, Abū al-Ḥasan 'Alī. *Dawr al-ḥadīth fī takwīn al-manākh al-islāmī wa ṣiyānatihī*. Lucknow, India: Nadwat al-'Ulamā'. 2nd edition. 1410/1989.

Nadwī, Abū al-Ḥasan ʿAlī. *The Glory of Iqbal.* UK: Awakening Publications, 2002.

Nadwī, Abū al-Ḥasan ʿAlī. *Ḥadīth Status and Role: An Introduction to the Prophet's Tradition.* Leicester, UK: UK Islamic Academy. 1426/2005.

Nadwī, Abū al-Ḥasan ʿAlī. *Idhā habbat rīḥ al-īmān.* Raebareli, India: Dār ʿArafāt. 1989.

Nadwī, Abū al-Ḥasan ʿAlī. *Life Sketch of Syed Ahmed Shahid.* Lucknow, India: Zia Publications. 1394/1974.

Nadwī, Abū al-Ḥasan ʿAlī. *Madhā khasira al-ʿālam bi inḥiṭāṭ al-muslimīn.* Egypt: Maktabat al-Īmān. n.d.

Nadwī, Abū al-Ḥasan ʿAlī. *Al-madkhal ilā dirāsāt al-ḥadīth al-nabawī al-sharīf.* Manṣūrah, Egypt: Dār al-Kalimah. 1418/1997.

Nadwī, Abū al-Ḥasan ʿAlī. *Mukhtārāt Min Adab al-ʿArab.* Damascus, Syria: Dār Ibn al-Kathīr. 1420/1999.

Nadwī, Abū al-Ḥasan ʿAlī. *Al-muslimūn fī al-hind.* Damascus, Syria: Dār Ibn al-Kathīr. 1420/1999.

Nadwī, Abū al-Ḥasan ʿAlī. *Rijāl al-fikr wa al-daʿwah.* Damascus, Syria: Dār Ibn Kathīr. 3rd edition. 1428/2007.

Nadwī, Abū al-Ḥasan ʿAlī. *Saviors of Islamic Spirit.* Karachi, Pakistan: Darul-Ishaat. 1994.

Nadwī, Abū al-Ḥasan ʿAlī. *Saviors of Islamic Spirit.* London, UK: White Thread Press. 2015.

Nadwī, Abū al-Ḥasan ʿAlī. *Sīrat Sayyid Aḥmad Shahīd.* Lucknow, India: Majlis Taḥqīqāt o Nashriyāt Islām. New edition. 1432/2011.

Nadwī, Abū al-Ḥasan ʿAlī. *Stories of the Prophets.* Leicester, UK: UK Islamic Academy. First published 1990. Revised 2011.

Nadwī, Moḥammad Akram. *Abū al-Ḥasan ʿAlī Nadwī: al-ʿālim al-murabbī wa al-dāʿiyat al-kabīr.* Damascus, Syria: Dār al-Qalam 1427/2006.

Nadwī, Moḥammad Akram. *Al-Fiqh al-Islāmī.* London, UK: Angelwing Media. 2012.

Nadwī, Moḥammad Akram. *Mabādiʾ al-naḥw.* London, UK: Al-Salam Institute Press. 1436/2015.

Nadwī, Moḥammad Akram. *Mabādiʾ al-taṣrīf.* London, UK: Al-Salam Institute Press. 1436/2015.

Nadwī, Moḥammad Akram. *Mabādiʾ fī ʿilm uṣūl al-fiqh.* London, UK: Al-Salam Institute Press. 1436/2015.

Nadwī, Moḥammad Akram. *Mabādiʾ fī ʿilm uṣūl al-tafsīr.* London, UK: Al-Salam Institute Press. 1436/2015.

Nadwī, Moḥammad Akram. *Mabādi' fī uṣūl al-ḥadīth wa al-isnād.* London, UK: Al-Salam Institute Press. 1436/2015.

Nadwī, Moḥammad Akram. *Madrasah Life: A Student's Day at Nadwat al-'Ulamā'.* London, UK: Turath Publishing. 1428/2007.

Nadwī, Moḥammad Akram. *Man 'Allamanī?* Lucknow, India: Dār al-Rashīd. 1440/2018.

Nadwī, Moḥammad Akram. *Shaykh Abū al-Ḥasan 'Alī Nadwī: His Life and Works.* West Yorkshire, UK: Nadwi Foundation. 1434/2013.

Nadwī, Nadhr al-Ḥafīẓ. *Abū al-Ḥasan al-Nadwī kātiban wa mufakkiran.* Kuwait: Dār al-Nashr wa al-Tawzī'. 1407/1986.

Sells, Michael A. *Desert Tracings: Six Classic Arabian Odes.* Connecticut, USA: Wesleyan University Press. 1989.

Smith, Paul. *The Seven Golden Odes of Arabia.* Australia: New Humanity Books. 2012.

Al-Shinqīṭī, Aḥmad al-Amīn. *Sharḥ al-Mu'allaqāt al-Sab'.* Beirut: Al-Maktabat al-'Aṣriyyah. 1434/2013.

Al-Ṭā'ī, Abū Tamām. *Dīwān al-ḥamāsah.* Beirut, Lebanon: Dār al-Kutub al-'Ilmiyyah. 1418/1998.

Al-Zawzanī, 'Abdullah al-Ḥasan. *Sharḥ al-Mu'allaqāt al-Sab'.* Beirut: Al-Maktabat al-'Aṣriyyah. 1434/2013.

INDEX

'Abd al-Fattāḥ Abū Ghuddah, v, 28, 30, 51, 54, 64, 68, 74, 83, 88, 95, 127, 130
'Abd al-Ḥayy, 146
'Abd al-Ḥayy al-Ḥasanī, 17, 18, 107
'Abd al-Nūr Nadwī, 122
'Abd al-Raḥmān Mubārakpūrī, 20, 22, 89
'Abd al-Sattār A'ẓamī, 89
Abū al-Dardā', 153
Abū al-Ḥasan 'Alī Nadwī, v, 1, 15, 30, 38, 39, 40, 49, 63, 64, 68, 74, 75, 100, 108, 113, 115, 119, 123, 126, 127, 130, 139, 162, 163
Abū al-'Irfān Nadwī, 90, 98, 100, 106, 110, 111, 115
Abū 'Ammār Zāhid Rāshidī, 104
Abū Naṣr al-Farābī, 103, 104, 161
Abū Tamīm, 109, 112
'Adnān, 137
Aḥmad Amīn, 106, 139
Aḥmad 'Āshūr, 151
Aḥmad Shawqī, 99
'Alam Allāh Barelvī, 17, 63, 68
'Alī b. al-Madīnī, 87, 151
'Alī Ṭanṭāwī, 114
'ālimiyyah degree, 7, 87
al-Rāzī, 81, 82, 93
anger, 6, 8, 33, 43, 59, 60, 61, 62, 63, 125, 131
'Antarah, 110, 161
Ash'arī, 157
Aurangzeb, 17, 38, 74
Bābrī Masjid, 62
Balakot, 17
Barelwī, 157
Bukhārī, 27, 28, 154
critical thinking, viii, 73, 103, 131
Dars-e-Niẓāmī curriculum, 104
da'wah, 17, 22, 24, 25, 28, 31, 75, 133, 158, 162
dialectics, 129
Dīwān al-Ḥamāsah, 112, 113
Ḍiyā' al-Dīn A'ẓamī, 128
Ḍiyā' al-Ḥasan Nadwī, 90
Dr. Bassam Saeh, 12
faḍīlah, 7
Faḍl al-Raḥmān Ganjmurādābādī, 38, 40
Farāhī, 1, 74, 76
Farewell Pilgrimage, 33
fear, viii, 8, 15, 43, 44, 45, 46, 47, 63, 97, 107, 125
fiqh, viii, 8, 75, 76, 83, 84, 87, 90, 94, 97, 101, 130, 162
forbearance, viii, 8, 59, 60, 61, 62, 63, 64
generosity of spirit, 23, 49, 50, 52
gentleness, 53, 54, 55, 56, 147
Ḥabīb al-Raḥmān Sulṭānpūrī, 98
ḥamāsah, 109, 112, 161, 163
Hārūn, 53
Ḥasan al-Ḥudaybī, 158
Ḥashmatullāh Nadwī, 108, 128
Ḥaydar Ḥasan Khān Ṭonkī, 19, 22, 32
history, 103
Ibn 'Arabī, 158
Ibn 'Aṭiyyah, 81
Ibn Khaldūn, 1, 105, 106, 115, 122, 137, 161

Ibn Taymiyyah, 1, 25, 47, 79, 80, 82, 107, 158, 161
Imām Bukhārī Conference in Samarqand, 27, 51, 130
Imām Muḥammad b. Sa'ūd Islamic University, 95, 123
Imra' al-Qays, 65, 109, 111
Industrial Revolution, 5
internet, 1, 2
Islamic schools, 5
Islamic thought, 67, 68, 70, 139
Jalīl Aḥsan Nadwī, 74
Jamā'at Islāmī, 158
Ka'b b. Zuhayr, 110
Khālid Barkat 'Alī, 128
literary criticism, 125
literary taste, 121
love for God, 24, 40
Lucknow, 145
Manners in Islam, 35
Mathnawī, 158
Māturīdī, 157
Mawdūdī, 1, 23, 24, 74, 158
Mawlānā Ashraf 'Alī Thānwī, 99
media and communication, 117
Mu'allaqāt, 109, 163
Muḍar, 137
Muḥammad Aḥmad of Pratapgarh, v, 38
Muḥammad 'Ārif Sunbhulī, 84
Muḥammad b. 'Alawī al-Mālikī, 31
Muḥammad Burhān al-Dīn Sunbhulī, 83
Muḥammad Rābi' Ḥasanī Nadwī, 61, 94, 111, 115, 116, 123, 126, 127
Muḥammad Wāḍiḥ Rashīd Nadwī, v, xi, 63, 68, 94, 124, 137, 151
Muḥammad Ẓahūr Nadwī, 94, 98, 100, 119
Muḥammad Zakariyyā Kāndihlawī, 64, 68, 69, 83, 92
Muḥammad Zakariyyā Sunbhulī, 91
Mukhtārāt Min Adab al-'Arab, 113, 115, 116, 162
musalsal, 64, 65, 69, 83, 127
Muṣṭafā Sibā'ī, 25, 139
Muṭarrif, 43
Nadhīr Ḥusayn Dihlawī, 19, 20, 89
Nadhr al-Ḥafīẓ Nadwī: Teachers, 119
Nāṣir 'Alī Nadwī, 94, 129
Niẓāmī curriculum, 104
Oxford, x, 3, 5, 11, 12, 15, 23, 27, 64, 69, 88, 157
passing of the scholars, 33
Pharaoh, 53, 135
pre-Islamic poetry, 109, 110, 111
principles of ḥadīth, 93
Prophet Ibrāhīm, 16, 60, 135
Prophet Ismā'īl, 59
Prophet Mūsā, 53
Prophet Yūsuf, 36, 80
Quraysh, 17, 137
Radio India, 68
Reciting the Qur'ān, 37
Rūmī, 158
Ṣadr al-Dīn Iṣlāḥī, 74
Ṣaḥīḥ Bukhārī, 17, 27, 33, 38, 46, 56, 83, 87, 89, 90, 91, 94, 100, 115, 119, 129
Sa'īd al-Raḥmān A'ẓamī, 94, 119, 126
Sa'īd b. Jubayr, 44
Sa'īd Ḥawwā, 54
Salmān Ḥusaynī Nadwī, 94
Sayyid Aḥmad Shahīd, 17, 19, 20, 24, 162
Sayyid Quṭb, 1, 24, 26, 158
sciences of tools and means, 7
Shafīq al-Raḥmān Nadwī, 113
Shāh Ismā'īl, 84
Shahbāz Iṣlāḥī, 74, 83, 87, 88
Shams al-Ḥaqq Nadwī, 115
Shiblī Nu'mānī, ix, 1, 106, 157

Siyar a'lām al-nubalā', 22, 44, 45, 88, 94, 161
study, 1
Sufyān al-Thawrī, 44, 152, 153
Ṭabarī, 81, 105
Tablīghī Jamā'ah, 24, 158
tafsīr, 79
Tafsīr of Ibn Kathīr, 81
Ṭāhā Ḥusayn, 139
Ṭarafah b. al-'Abd, 3, 65, 124
ta'wīl, 79
Tīlī Wālī Masjid, 38
waḥdat al-wujūd, 158
WhatsApp, 1, 2
writing an article, 141
Yaḥyā b. Sa'īd al-Anṣārī, 28
YouTube, 1, 2
Yūsuf al-Qaraḍāwī, 30
Zamakhsharī, 82, 120